Thai for Lovers

by

Nit & Jack Ajee
นิดกับแจ๊ค อาจี

A Complete Guide to the Romantic Culture of Thailand

PAIBOON
PP
PUBLISHING

ภาษาไทยสำหรับคู่รัก

- 299 BAHT -

Thai for Lovers

Copyright ©1999 by Paiboon Publishing

(สำนักพิมพ์ไพบูลย์ภูมิแสน)

Printed in Thailand

All rights reserved

Paiboon Poomsan Publishing
582 Amarinniwate Village 2
Sukhapiban Road 1, Bungkum
Bangkok 10230
THAILAND
☎   662-509-8632
Fax 662-519-5437

Paiboon Publishing
PMB 192, 1442A Walnut Street
Berkeley, California USA 94709
☎   1-510-848-7086
Fax 1-510-848-4521
E-Mail: paiboon@thailao.com
www.thailao.com

สำนักพิมพ์ไพบูลย์ภูมิแสน
582 หมู่บ้านอัมรินทร์นิเวศน์ 2
ถ. สุขาภิบาล 1 เขตบึงกุ่ม
ก.ท.ม. 10230
☎   662-509-8632
โทรสาร 662-519-5437

paiboon@thailao.com
www.thailao.com

Cover and graphic design by Randy Kincaid
Edited by Craig Becker, Benjawan Becker and Tim McDaniel
Cartoons by Addissapong Praphantanathorn

ISBN 1-887521-04-6

Introduction

Thai for Lovers offers a new and fun way to communicate in Thai. Most books on the Thai language are either serious academic works or traditional language guides which help visitors navigate restaurants, airports, hotels and so forth. *Thai for Lovers* is the Thai language book which readers have been waiting for! It serves as an ideal language and cultural guide to one of the most fascinating journeys of all— cross-cultural romance. The reader will learn simple words, phrases and explanations to use in the romantic liaison of his or her choice. No prior experience with Thai is necessary. Short cultural commentaries and language explanations add spice to each chapter. An accurate and easy to follow pronunciation guide appears at the beginning of the book and there is a Thai translation for every sentence in the text. For a general Thai language textbook we suggest that you refer to *Thai for Beginners*.

The country's beauty and the legendary friendliness of the Thai people have made Thailand one of the world's favorite destinations. Many travelers return time after time and end up developing a romantic relationship with a Thai woman or man. Since most Thai people do not speak English fluently, a little knowledge of Thai language and culture can be indispensable. What better motivation to learn than the pursuit of romance?

In fact, based on our experience teaching foreign languages in Thailand, Japan, the United States and Mexico we developed the Psycho-Sexual Theory of Language Acquisition: "In inverse proportion to a foreign language's cultural and economic impact on the world, adults are motivated to study it in direct proportion to their sexual attraction for the native speakers of that language." For example, there are many cultural and economic reasons to study Japanese, German and Spanish. There are fewer reasons to study Finnish, Hungarian and Thai. The peoples and cultures of these countries are fascinating, but they are smaller markets. When we scratched the surface we found that most students who were serious about studying Thai were doing so to pursue a romantic relationship. Of course, there are exceptions, such as the dedicated student of Thai Buddhism or the worker moving to Thailand, but the exceptions were few.

Nit has been asked the same questions over and over while teaching Thai in Japan and the United States. People wanted to know what words and phrases to use, the differences between formal and informal language, how to express feelings in Thai, and Thai attitudes towards love and romance.

This book provides the answers to these and many other questions you may have had. We have tried to make it enjoyable, easy to read and as useful to you as possible. Please email your comments to: paiboon@thailao.com. Good luck!

ขอให้โชคดี

Table of Contents

Guide to Pronunciation

Tones

Because Thai is a tonal language, its pronunciation presents new challenges for English speakers. If the tone is wrong, you will not be easily understood even if everything else is correct. Thai uses five tones. For example, to pronounce a rising tone, your voice starts at a low pitch and goes up (much like asking a question in English). The phonetic transliteration in this text book uses tone marks over the vowels to show the tone for each word. Note that the tone marks used for transliteration are different from those used in Thai script.

Tone Marks (Transliteration)

Tone	Tone symbol	Example
mid	*None*	maa
low	`	màa
falling	^	mâa
high	´	máa
rising	ˇ	mǎa

Vowels

Most Thai vowels have two versions, short and long. Short vowels are clipped and cut off at the end. Long ones are drawn out. This book shows short vowels with a single letter and long vowels with double letters ('a' for short; 'aa' for long).

The 'ʉ' has no comparable sound in English. Try saying 'u' while spreading your lips in as wide a smile as possible. If the sound you are making is similar to one you might have uttered after stepping on something disgusting, you are probably close!

Short & Long Vowels

a	*like a in Alaska*	fan - *teeth*
aa	*like a in father*	maa - *come*
i	*like i in tip*	sìp - *ten*
ii	*like ee in see*	sìi - *four*
u	*like oo in boot*	kun - *you*
uu	*like u in ruler*	sǔun - *zero*
ʉ	*like u in ruler, but with a smile*	nʉ̀ng - *one*
ʉʉ	*like ʉ but longer*	mʉʉ - *hand*
e	*like e in pet*	sèt - *finish*
ee	*like a in pale*	pleeng-*song*
ε	*like a in cat*	lέ - *and*
εε	*like a in sad*	dεεng - *red*
ə	*like er in teacher without the r sound*	lə́ - *dirty*
əə	*like ə but longer*	jəə - *meet*
o	*like o in note*	jon - *poor*
oo	*like o in go*	joon -*robber*
ɔ	*like au in caught*	gɔ̀ - *island*
ɔɔ	*like aw in law*	nɔɔn - *sleep*

Complex Vowels

The following dipthongs are combinations of the above vowels.

ai	mâi - *not*		aai	saai - *sand*
ao	mao - *drunk*		aao	kâao - *rice*
ia	bia - *beer*		iao	nǐao - *sticky*
ua	dtua- *body*		uai	ruai - *rich*
ʉa	rʉa - *boat*		ʉai	nʉ̀ai - *tired*
ɔi	nɔ̀i - *little*		ɔɔi	kɔɔi - *wait*
ooi	dooi - *by*		əəi	nəəi - *butter*
ui	kui - *chat*		iu	hǐu - *hungry*
eo	reo - *fast*		eeo	eeo - *waist*
εo	tɛ̌o - *row*		εεo	lέεo - *already*

Consonants

b	*as in* <u>b</u>aby	bin - *fly*
ch	*as in* <u>ch</u>in	chûu - *name*
d	*as in* <u>d</u>oll	duu - *look*
f	*as in* <u>f</u>un	fai - *fire*
g	*as in* <u>g</u>old	gin - *eat*
h	*as in* <u>h</u>oney	hâa - *five*
j	*as in* <u>j</u>et	jèt - *seven*
k	*as in* <u>k</u>iss	kon - *person*
l	*as in* <u>l</u>ove	ling - *monkey*
m	*as in* <u>m</u>oney	mii - *have*
n	*as in* <u>n</u>eed	naa - *rice field*
p	*as in* <u>p</u>retty	pan - *thousand*
r	*rolled like the Scottish* <u>r</u>	rian - *study*
s	*as in* <u>s</u>ex	sìi - *four*
t	*as in* <u>t</u>ender	tam - *do*
w	*as in* <u>w</u>oman	wan - *day*
y	*as in* <u>y</u>ou	yaa - *medicine*
ng	*as in* ri<u>ng</u>ing	ngaan - *work*
dt	*as in* s<u>t</u>op	dtaa - *eye*
bp	*as in* s<u>p</u>ot	bpai - *go*

The /dt/ sound lies between the /d/ and the /t/. Similarly, the /bp/ is between /b/ and /p/. (In linguistic terms, they are both unvoiced and unaspirated.) Unlike English, /ng/ frequently occurs at the beginning of words in Thai. Thai people often do not pronounce the /r/, replacing it with /l/ ('rian' will sound like 'lian'). When the /r/ is part of a consonant cluster, it is often dropped completely. ('kráp' will sound like 'káp'.)

Tips on Using This Book...

◆ Read the introduction and guide to pronunciation— they will help you use the rest of the book more effectively.

◆ Have a Thai read some sentences for you and try to imitate the sounds.

or...

◆ Just find the sentence in the book that you want to say and point to it.

◆ Take this book with you and your conversations with Thai friends will be more fun than ever before!

CHAPTER ONE

Greetings

"A smile is the chosen vehicle of all ambiguities."
—HERMAN MELVILLE, *Pierre*

Thai Smiles

It won't take long for you to see why Thailand is called "The Land of Smiles". So limber up those facial muscles! In Thailand a smile is an essential part of greeting and interacting with people. It can mean virtually anything from "Hello, I'm so happy to see you" to "I'm sorry" to "I'm angry at you but at least I'll be polite". The Thai people's hospitality is second to none and at first most visitors bask in the warm glow of friendly smiles. It seems that everyone likes you and wants to be your friend! Sometimes people get a bit cynical later on—perhaps they have had a negative experience or two— and begin to think that the Thai smile is hypocritical. Neither attitude is really accurate. Smiling is simply considered the proper way for a Thai to present himself to the world under almost all circumstances. When you are smiled at, don't forget to smile back or you may be perceived as being rude and unfriendly.

◆   Good morning.   sa-wàtdii (kráp/kâ)
    Good afternoon.   สวัสดี (ครับ/ค่ะ)
    Good evening.
    Hello.
    Goodbye.

Note: sà-watdii is the all purpose word for greeting and leave taking. The speaker decides whether to use the polite particle kráp (for male speakers) or kâ (for female speakers) depending on the level of politeness. The phrase is used as follows:

sa-wàtdii kráp.   สวัสดีครับ (men)
sa-wàtdii kâ.   สวัสดีค่ะ (women)

When you want to be polite (most of the time), add kráp or kâ at the end of sentences. kráp or kâ are also used when answering a question in the affirmative, as an acknowledgement when called or spoken to and as a particle placed after a name, title or kin term to address or attract the attention of someone.

◆   Hello.   wàtdii.
                                         หวัดดี

This is a short version of sa-watdii which is very common now for informal use among close friends, people who know each other well and young people. It's OK for foreigners to use in informal speach. It will sound cute to the Thai ear. Just don't forget to add the polite particle kráp or kâ.

◆ How are you?   sa-baai-dii mái?
                                   สบายดีมั้ย?

   ● Fine.   sa-baai-dii.
                                   สบายดี

   ● So-so.   rûai-rûai.
                                   เรื่อยๆ

   ● Not so good.   mâi kɔ̂i sa-baai.
                                   ไม่ค่อยสบาย

   ● I have a headache.   bpùat hǔa.
                                   ปวดหัว

◆ How have you been doing?   bpen ngai bâang?
                                   เป็นไงบ้าง?
                                   bpen ngai?
                                   เป็นไง?

◆ How are things going?   bpen yang ngai?
                                   เป็นยังไง?

   ● Pretty good.   gɔ̂ɔ dii.
                                   ก็ดี

   ● Not so good.   mâi kɔ̂i dii tâo-rài.
                                   ไม่ค่อยดีเท่าไหร่

   ● Not bad.   mâi leeo.
                                   ไม่เลว

◆ Where are you going?*   bpai nǎi?
                                   ไปไหน?

   ● Shopping.   bpai súu kɔ̌ɔng.
                                   ไปซื้อของ

- I'm going out to have fun.   bpai fiao.
  ไปเที่ยว

- No where.   mâi bpai năi.
  ไม่ไปไหน

◆ Where have you been?*   bpai năi maa?
  ไปไหนมา?

  - Out shopping.   bpai súu-kɔ̌ɔng (maa).
    ไปซื้อของ (มา)

  - Out having fun.   bpai fiao (maa).
    ไปเที่ยว (มา)

◆ Have you eaten?*   gin kâao rú yang?
  กินข้าวหรือยัง?

  - Yes.   gin lέɛo.
    กินแล้ว

  - Not yet.   yang mâi gin.
    ยังไม่ได้กิน

*Note: It may seem to you that Thai people are overly curious about where you are going, where you have been and whether you have eaten or not. Actually, these questions are often just another way of saying "hello". Don't feel obligated to give a detailed itinerary— the asker may not really care about the answer anyway.

◆ Long time no see   mâi dâai jɔɔ tâng naan.
  ไม่ได้เจอตั้งนาน

◆ I'm glad you dropped by.   dii-jai fii kun maa.
  (I'm glad you came to see me.)   ดีใจที่คุณมาหา

◆ How's business?   tu-ra-gìt bpen yang-ngai?

                                  ธุรกิจเป็นยังไง?

● Okay, I suppose.   kít-wâa dii.

                                    คิดว่าดี

● Not bad.   mâi leeo.

                                    ไม่เลว

◆ Welcome.   choon kráp/kâ.

                                    เชิญครับ/ ค่ะ

◆ Sweet dreams.   fǎn dii (ná) .

                                    ฝันดี(นะ)

Note: ná (นะ) is a particle commonly used at the end of a sentence to make a statement softer and gentler or to be persuasive, suggestion or asking for agreement.

◆ See you tomorrow.   joo-gan prûng-nii (ná).

                                    เจอกันพรุ่งนี้ (นะ)

◆ See you later.   joo-gan mài (ná).

                                    เจอกันใหม่ (นะ)

◆ Thank you.   kɔɔpkun kráp/kâ.

                                    ขอบคุณครับ/ ค่ะ

◆ Excuse me./I'm sorry.   kɔ̌ɔ-tôot (ná).

                                    ขอโทษ(นะ)

                                    kɔ̌ɔ-tôot kráp/kâ.

                                    ขอโทษครับ/ ค่ะ

                                        tôot-tii.
                                        โทษที (colloquial)

◆ Never mind.   mâi-bpen-rai kráp/kâ.
    You're welcome.   ไม่เป็นไรครับ/ค่ะ

Note: mâi-bpen-rai also has the following meaings: it doesn't
matter; that's all right; not at all; it's nothing; don't mention it;
forget it, etc.

◆ What's your name?   kun chûu a-rai (kráp/ká)?
                                        คุณชื่ออะไร (ครับ/ คะ)?

  ● My name is John.   (pŏm) chûu jɔɔn (kráp).
                                        (ผม) ชื่อจอห์น (ครับ)

  ● My name is Judy.   (chán) chûu juu-ɗii (kâ).
                                        (ฉัน) ชื่อจูดี้ (ค่ะ)

Note: pŏm (ผม) means "I" for male speakers, and chán (ฉัน)
(informal) or di-chán (ดิฉัน) (more formal) is for female speakers.
Sometimes the pronouns are omitted when the context is clear.

◆ What kind of work do you do?   kun tam-ngaan a-rai?
                                        คุณทำงานอะไร?
                                        kun mii aa-chîip a-rai?
                                        คุณมีอาชีพอะไร?

  ● I'm a businessperson.   pŏm/chán bpen nák
                                           tu-ra-gìt kráp/kâ.
                                        (ผม/ฉัน) เป็นนักธุรกิจ (ครับ/ ค่ะ)

You can replace the underlined word with the following:

Professions:

actor	nák sa-dɛɛng นักแสดง
ambassador	tûut ทูต
artist	sĭnla-bpin ศิลปิน
athlete	nák gii-laa นักกีฬา
bar girl	pûu-yĭng baa ผู้หญิงบาร์
bartender	baa-ten-dɔ̂ɔ บาร์เทนเดอร์
broker	naai-nâa นายหน้า
company employee	pa-nák-ngaan bɔɔ-ri-sàt พนักงานบริษัท
cook	gúk, kon tam aa-hăan กุ๊ก, คนทำอาหาร
dancer	nák dtên นักเต้น
dentist	mɔ̆ɔ fan หมอฟัน
doctor	mɔ̆ɔ หมอ
driver	kon kàp-rót คนขับรถ
engineer	wítsa-wá-gɔɔn วิศวกร
farmer	chaao-naa ชาวนา
flight attendant	sa-júat, ɛɛ-hótsa-teet สจ๊วต, แอร์โฮสเตท
go-go dancer	nák dtên a-goo-gôo นักเต้นอะโกโก้
government offical	kâa-râatcha-gaan ข้าราชการ
housewife	mɛ̂ɛ-bâan แม่บ้าน
lawyer	ta-naai-kwaam ทนายความ
masseuse masseur	mɔ̆ɔ nûat หมอนวด
musician	nák don-dtrii นักดนตรี
nurse	pa-yaa-baan พยาบาล

pilot	gàp-dtan krûang-bin กัปตันเครื่องบิน
policeman, policewoman	dtamrùat ตำรวจ
professor	aa-jaan อาจารย์
prostitute	soo-pee-nee โสเภณี
retired from work	ga-sĭan เกษียณ
salesperson	pa-nák-ngaan kăai พนักงานขาย
secretary	lee-kăa เลขา
self-employed	tu-ra-gìt sŭan-dtua ธุรกิจส่วนตัว
shop owner	jâao-kɔ̆ɔng ráan เจ้าของร้าน
singer	nák rɔ́ɔng นักร้อง
soldier	ta-hăan ทหาร
student	nák rian นักเรียน
student (in college)	nák sùksăa นักศึกษา
taxi-driver	kon kàp ték-sîi คนขับแท็กซี่
teacher	kruu, aa-jaan ครู, อาจารย์
tourist	nák tông-tîao นักท่องเที่ยว
unemployed	dtòk-ngaan ตกงาน
veterinarian	sàt-dta-wa-pêet สัตวแพทย์
volunteer	aa-săa sa-màk อาสาสมัคร
writer	nák kĭan นักเขียน

◆ What country are you from?   kun maa jàak bpra-têet arai?
                                   คุณมาจากประเทศอะไร?

● I'm from America.   (maa) jàak <u>a-mee-ri-gaa</u>
                                   (kráp/kâ).
                                   (มา) จาก<u>อเมริกา</u> (ครับ/ ค่ะ)

Some Country Names:

America	a-mee-ri-gaa อเมริกา
Argentina	aa-jen-dti-nâa อาร์เจนตินา
Australia	ɔ́ɔt-sa-dtee-lia ออสเตรเลีย
Austria	ɔ́ɔt-sa-dtria ออสเตรีย
Belgium	ben-yîam เบลเยี่ยม
Brazil	braa-sin บราชิล
Burma	pá-mâa พม่า
Cambodia	ka-měen เขมร
Canada	kɛnnaa-daa แคนาดา
China	jiin จีน
Colombia	koo-lambia โคลัมเบีย
Denmark	denmàak เดนมาร์ก
Egypt	ii-yǐp อียิปต์
England	ang-grĭt อังกฤษ
Finland	fin-lɛɛn ฟินแลนด์
France	fa-ràng-sèet ฝรั่งเศส
Germany	yɔɔ-ra-man เยอรมัน
Greece	grĭik กรีก
India	india อินเดีย
Indonesia	indo-nii-sia อินโดนีเซีย
Iran	ǐ-ràan อิหร่าน
Iraq	ǐ-rák อิรัค
Ireland	ai-lɛɛn ไอแลนด์
Israel	ǐtsa-raa-eo อิสราเอล
Italy	ǐt-dtaa-lǐi อิตาลี
Japan	yîi-bpùn ญี่ปุ่น
Korea	gao-lǐi เกาหลี
Laos	laao ลาว

Malaysia	maa-lee-sia มาเลเซีย
Mexico	méksi-goo เม็กซิโก
Nepal	nee-paan เนปาล
Netherlands	nee-təə-lɛɛn เนเธอร์แลนด์
Norway	nɔɔ-ra-wee นอรเวย์
New Zealand	niu-sii-lɛɛn นิวซีแลนด์
Pakistan	bpaa-gii-sa-tǎan ปากีสถาน
Protugal	bproo-dtu-gèet โปรตุเกส
Phillipines	fi-li-bpin ฟิลลิปินส์
Russia	rátsia รัสเซีย
Saudi Arabia	saa-u ซาุ
Scotland	sa-gótlɛɛn สก็อตแลนด์
Singapore	sǐng-ka-poo สิงคโปร์
Spain	sa-bpeen สเปน
Sweden	sa-wii-den สวีเดน
Switzerland	sa-wítsəə-lɛɛn สวิสเซอร์แลนด์
Taiwan	dtâi-wǎn ได้หวัน
Turkey	dtu-ra-gii ตุรกี
Thailand	mɯang tai เมืองไทย
	bpra-têet tai ประเทศไทย
Vietnam	wîat-naam เวียดนาม

◆ What nationality are you? — kun bpen kon châat a-rai?
คุณเป็นคนชาติอะไร?

● I'm American. — (pǒm/chán)
bpen kon a-mee ri-gan
(ผม/ฉัน) เป็นคนอเมริกัน

● I'm Japanese — (pǒm/chán)
bpen kon yii-bpùn.
(ผม/ฉัน) เป็นคนญี่ปุ่น

◆ Are you a tourist?   kun bpen nák tông-fiao

                                             châi mái?

                                     คุณเป็นนักท่องเที่ยวใช่ไหม?

● Yes, I am.   châi kráp/kâ

                                     ใช่ครับ/ค่ะ

● No I'm a business person.   mâi-châi kráp/kâ.

                                     ไม่ใช่ครับ/ค่ะ

                                     pŏm/chán bpen nák

                                       tu-ra-gìt.

                                     ผม/ฉันเป็นนักธุรกิจ

"Wâi" ไหว้

One of the most important aspects of greeting people in Thailand is the *wai*. Generally, you put your hands together in front of your chest and bend your head. The higher your hands and the lower you bow your head, the more respect you show. There are four levels of wai in general use as follows:

1.   To *wai* a monk or statue of Lord Buddha

Put your hands together, with both your thumbs between the eyebrows and bend your head and neck as much as you can. You don't need to bend your body very much Monks, by the way, do not *wai* back to lay people.

You can also put your hands on the floor and touch your forhead to your hands. This is called a "graap" (กราบ). You only *graap* monks or statues of Lord Buddha.

2.   To *wai* parents or teachers

Put your hands together with both thumbs near the tip of your nose and bend your head and neck about 45 degrees, not as low as when you *wai* a monk.

3.   To *wai* people in general, relatives and older people

Put your hands together with both thumbs near the tip of your chin and bend your head and neck about 20-25 degrees. This is a very common way to *wai* and is the one that you should use most of the time. In fact, if you don't know any of the other *wai*s, just use this one with everybody and you should do fine.

4.   To *wai* people younger or of lower status than you

You do this to accept a wai from children or from somebody of lower status than yourself. Put your hands together near your chest and bend your head very slightly. Be careful not to bend your head too low, or else you will look a bit silly. By the way, you shouldn't wai at all if the younger person doesn't wai you first. The same goes with someone of obviously lower status. For example, you would never wai first to a waiter seating you in a restaurant or to a doorman at a hotel. In these circumstances, when there is no wai forthcoming, giving a friendly and polite smile is all you need do.

Thailand is a very status conscious society and the *wai* is generally used as a way of showing respect to someone of higher or equal status. The higher status person than returns or acknowledges the wai.

Some Basic Thai Words and Phrases

This.   nîi.
                                               นี่

What's this?   nîi a-rai?
                                               นี่อะไร?

That.   nân.
                                               นั่น

What's that?

nân a-rai?
นั่นอะไร?

Here.

tii-nîi.
ที่นี่

There.

tii-nân
ที่นั้น

What?

a-rai?
อะไร

Who?

krai?
ใคร

Whose?

kɔ̌ɔng-krai?
ของใคร?

Where?

tii-nǎi?
ที่ไหน?

When?

mɯ̂a-rài?
เมื่อไหร่?

Why?

tammai?
ทำไม?

How?

yang-ngai?/yàang-rai?
ยังไง?/ อย่างไร?

How much?

tâo-rài?
เท่าไหร่?

Really?	jing-rɔ̌ə? จริงเหรอ?
Really.	jing-jing. จริงๆ
Yes.	châi. ใช่
No.	mâi-châi. ไม่ใช่
If.	tâa. ถ้า
But.	dtὲε. แต่
Because.	prɔ́-wâa. เพราะว่า
Don't.	yàa. อย่า
Don't do it.	yàa tam. อย่าทำ
O.K.	oo-kee/dtòk-long. โอเค/ตกลง

So-so.	tamma-daa/chǒǝi-chǒǝi. ธรรมดา/เฉยๆ
Maybe.	bang-tii/àat-jà. บางที/อาจจะ
Please.	ga-ru-naa, bp̀ròot. กรุณา, โปรด
Thank you.	kɔ̀ɔp-kun. ขอบคุณ
You're welcome.	mâi-bpen-rai. ไม่เป็นไร
Good-bye.	báai-baai/laa-gɔ̀ɔn. บ้ายบาย/ลาก่อน
Nice to meet you.	yindii ทii-dâai rúu-jàk. ยินดีที่ได้รู้จัก
My name is _____ (male).	pǒm chน̂น _____. ผมชื่อ _____
My name is _____ (female).	chán chน̂น _____. ฉันชื่อ _____
Where are you from?	kun maa jàak nǎi? คุณมาจากไหน?

What country are you from?	kun maa jàak bpra-têet a-rai? คุณมาจากประเทศอะไร?
I'm from _____.	pŏm/chán maa jàak _____. ผม/ฉันมาจาก _____
I'm (nationality).	pŏm/chán bpen kon _____. ผม/ฉันเป็นคน _____
I'm Japanese.	pŏm/chán bpen kon yîi-bpùn. ผม/ฉันเป็นคนญี่ปุ่น
How old are you?	kun aa-yú tâo-rài? คุณอายุเท่าไหร่?
I'm _____ years old.	pŏm/chán aa-yú _____ bpii. ผม/ฉันอายุ _____ ปี
Where do you live?	kun yùu tîi năi? คุณอยู่ที่ไหน?

Look for more words and phrases that express needs and feelings in Chapter 3.

CHAPTER TWO
General Conversation

"There is no such thing as conversation. It is an illusion. There are intersecting monologues, that is all." —REBECCA WEST, *There Is No Conversation*

◆ Do you like Thailand?

(kun) chɔ̂ɔp mɯang tai mái?

(คุณ) ชอบเมืองไทยมั้ย?

  ● Yes, very much.

chɔ̂ɔp mâak.

ชอบมาก

  ● Not so much.

mâi-kɔ̂i chɔ̂ɔp tâo-rài.

ไม่ค่อยชอบเท่าไหร่

◆ Do you like Thai food?

(kun) chɔ̂ɔp aa-hǎan tai mái?

(คุณ) ชอบอาหารไทยมั้ย?

  ● Yes, very much.

chɔ̂ɔp mâak.

ชอบมาก

● Yes, I think it's very good.   chɔ̂ɔp, kít wâa a-rɔ̀i mâak.
                                  ชอบ คิดว่าอร่อยมาก

● I think it's too spicy for me. kít wâa pèt gəən bpai.
                                  คิดวาเผ็ดเกินไป

◆ What do you think about   (kun) kít-wâa mɯang tai
    Thailand?   bpen yang-ngai?
                                  (คุณ) คิดวาเมืองไทยเป็นยังไง?

   ● I think it's very beautiful. kít-wâa sǔai mâak.
                                   คิดว่าสวยมาก

   ● I think it's a hard place   kít-wâa mâi nâa yùu.
       to live in.   คิดว่าไม่น่าอยู่

   ● I think it's very hot.   kít-wâa rɔ́ɔn mâak.
                                   คิดว่าร้อนมาก

◆ I like Bangkok.   (pǒm/chán) chɔ̂ɔp
                                     grung-têep.
                                  (ผม/ฉัน) ชอบกรุงเทพฯ

◆ I don't like Bangkok.   (pǒm/chán) mâi chɔ̂ɔp
                                     grung-têep.
                                  (ผม/ฉัน) ไม่ชอบกรุงเทพฯ

◆ Bangkok's traffic is terrible. grung-têep rót-dtìt mâak.
                                  กรุงเทพฯ รถติดมาก

◆ What do you think about   (kun) kít-wâa kon tai
    Thai people?   bpen yang-ngai?
                                  (คุณ) คิดว่าคนไทยเป็นยังไง?

   ● I think they are nice.   kít-wâa kon tai nâa-rák.
                                   คิดว่าคนไทยน่ารัก

◆ What do you think about me? (kun) kít-wâa pŏm/chán
bpen yang-ngai?
(คุณ) คิดว่าผม/ฉันเป็นยังไง?

● I think you are very nice. kít-wâa kun <u>nâa-rák</u> mâak.
คิดว่าคุณน่ารักมาก

You can replace the underline words with adjectives. (See p. 39.)

◆ Can you speak Thai? kun pûut tai dâai mái?
(คุณ) พูดไทยได้มั้ย?

● Not at all. mâi dâai leei.
ไม่ได้เลย

● A little bit. nítnɔ̀i.
นิดหน่อย

● Yes, but not very well. dâai, dtὲɛ mâi gèng.
ได้ แต่ไม่เก่ง

● Pretty well. pùut dâai geng mâak.
พูดได้เก่งมาก

◆ Where did you learn Thai? kun rian paa-săa tai fii-năi?
คุณเรียนภาษาไทยที่ไหน?

● With a Thai teacher in rian gàp kruu kon taɪ naɪ
America. a-mee-ri-gaa.
เรียนกับครูคนไทยในอเมริกา

● From this book. jàak năngsŭɯ lêm níi.
จากหนังสือเล่มนี้

● By myself. rian dûai dtua-eeng.
เรียนด้วยตัวเอง

◆ You speak Thai very well.   คุณพูดภาษาไทยเก่งมาก
                               kun pûut paa-săa tai
                                   gèng mâak.

◆ You speak English very well. kun pûut paa-săa anggrìt
                                   gèng mâak.
                               คุณพูดภาษาอังกฤษเก่งมาก

◆ Really?   jing rǔu kráp/ká?
                               จริงหรือครับ/คะ?

◆ Thank you.   kɔ̀ɔpkun kráp/kâ.
                               ขอบคุณครับ/ค่ะ

◆ Where are you from?   kun maa jàak năi?
                               คุณมาจากไหน?

   ● I'm from America.   pŏm/chán maa jàak
                                   a-mee-ri-gaa.
                               ผม/ฉันมาจากอเมริกา

● My hometown is Chiangmai.   bâan pŏm/chán yùu tîi
                                   chiang-mài.
                               บ้านผม/ฉันอยู่ที่เชียงใหม่

◆ How many times have you   kun maa mɯang tai gìi
     been to Thailand?   kráng lɛ́ɛo?
                               คุณมาเมืองไทยกี่ครั้งแล้ว?

   ● First time.   kráng rɛ̂ɛk.
                               ครั้งแรก

   ● Six times already.   hòk kráng lɛ́ɛo.
                               หกครั้งแล้ว

- Many many times.

  lăai kráng léɛo.

  หลายครั้งแล้ว

- I don't remember.

  jam mâi dâai.

  จำไม่ได้

- I lost count.

  náp mâi tûan.

  นับไม่ถ้วน

◆ Where have you visited?

  kun bpai tiâo fii-năi bâang?

  คุณไปเที่ยวที่ไหนบ้าง?

- I've been to Bangkok and
  Pattaya.

  bpai grung-têep gàp
      pátta-yaa.

  ไปกรุงเทพกับพัทยา

- I've been to the North and
  the South.

  bpai pâak nŭa gàp
      pâak dtâai.

  ไปภาคเหนือและภาคใต้

- Many places.

  bpai lăai fii léɛo.

  ไปหลายที่แล้ว

◆ Where do you like the most?

  kun chɔ̂ɔp fii-năi mâak
      fii-sùt?

  คุณชอบที่ไหนมากที่สุด?

- I like Chiangmai the most.

  chɔ̂ɔp chiang-mai fii sùt.

  ชอบเชียงใหม่ที่สุด

- I like everywhere except
  Bangkok.

  chɔ̂ɔp tùk fii yôk-wén
      grung-têep.

  ชอบทุกที่ยกเว้นกรุงเทพ

◆ How do you say this in Thai?

  paa-săa tai rîak-wâa a-rai?

  ภาษาไทยเรียกว่าอะไร?

◆ What do you call this in Thai?   paa-săa tai rîak an-níi
                                    wâa a-rai?
                                    ภาษาไทยเรียกอันนี้ว่าอะไร?

◆ How do you read this in Thai?   an-níi paa-săa tai àan
                                    wâa a-rai?
                                    อันนี้ภาษาไทยอ่านว่าอะไร?

◆ What does this mean?   nîi bplɛɛ-wâa a-rai?
                                    นี่แปลว่าอะไร?

◆ What does ____ mean?   ____ bplɛɛ-wâa a-rai?
                                    ____ แปลว่าอะไร?

◆ How do you say ____ in Thai?   paa-săa tai rîak ____
                                    wâa a-rai?
                                    ภาษาไทยเรียก ____ ว่าอะไร?

◆ When did you arrive in   kun maa-tŭng mɯang tai
   Thailand?   mɯ̂a-rài?
                                    คุณมาถึงเมืองไทยเมื่อไหร่?

   ● I just arrived.   pɔ̂ng maa-tŭng.
                                    เพิ่งมาถึง

   ● I arrived last night.   maa-tŭng mɯ̂a-kɯɯn níi.
                                    มาถึงเมื่อคืนนี้

   ● I've been here for   maa dâai nɯ̀ng dɯan lɛ́ɛo
     one month.   มาได้หนึ่งเดือนแล้ว

◆ Do you have brothers and   kun mii pîi-nɔ́ɔng máɪ?
   sisters?   คุณมีพี่น้องไหม?

◆ How many brothers and sisters do you have?

kun mii pîi-nɔ̂ng gìi kon.

คุณมีพี่น้องกี่คน?

● I have one older brother and two younger sisters.

mii pîi-chaai nùng kon gàp nɔ́ɔng-sǎao sɔ̌ɔng kon.

มีพี่ชายหนึ่งคนกับน้องสาวสองคน

● I'm the only child.

pǒm/chán bpen lûuk kon diao.

ผม/ฉันเป็นลูกคนเดียว

◆ I'm the oldest child.

pǒm bpen lûuk kon dtoo.

ผมเป็นลูกคนโต

◆ I'm the second child.

pǒm bpen lûuk kon tîi-sɔ̌ɔng.

ผมเป็นลูกคนที่สอง

◆ I'm the youngest child.

pǒm bpen lûuk kon sùt tɔ́ɔng.

ผมเป็นลูกคนสุดท้อง

◆ How old are you?

(kun) aa-yú tâo-rài?

(คุณ) อายุเท่าไหร่?

● I'm thirty.

sǎam-sìp.

สามสิบ

● Guess!

taai duu sì!

ทายดูสิ!

● I'm not going to tell you.

mâi bɔ̀k.

ไม่บอก

● Not so old.

mâi gὲε tâo-rài.

ไม่แก่เท่าไหร่

hen is your birthday?

wan gòət kun mùa-rài?

วันเกิดคุณเมื่อไหร่?

◆ Do you have a
boyfriend/girlfriend?

kun mii fɛɛn rɨ́ yang?

คุณมีแฟนหรือยัง?

● Yes, I do.

mii lɛ́ɛo.

มีแล้ว

● Not yet.

yang mâi-mii.

ยังไม่มี

● I haven't found one yet.

yang hǎa mâi jəə.

ยังหาไม่เจอ

● I have many.

mii yɔ́-yɛ́.

มีเยอะแยะ

● Why do you ask?

taam tammai?

ถามทำไม?

What's a fɛɛn ?

The word fɛɛn (แฟน) probably comes from the English word "fan" but in Thai it doesn't only refer to a sports enthusiast or the follower of a rock star. When somebody is referred to as a fɛɛn, it can mean a lover, a wife, a husband, a boyfriend, a girlfriend or a fiancé(e). If you want to know more specifically which, you have to guess from the context or simply ask politely whether or not someone is married or engaged to their fɛɛn.

◆ Are you dating anybody?

(kun) mii dèet gàp krai
yùu rɨ̌ɨ bplào?

(คุณ) มีเดทกับใครอยู่หรือเปล่า?

- Yes.

  mii lέεo.

  มีแล้ว

- I wish I were.

  tâa mii gɔ̂ɔ dii sĭ.

  ถ้ามีก็ดีสิ

- I don't have a boyfriend/
  girlfriend yet.

  yang mâi mii fεεn.

  ยังไม่มีแฟน

◆ Are you married?

  (kun) dtὲng-ngaan rɯ́ yang?

  (คุณ) แต่งงานรึยัง?

- Yes, I am.

  dtὲng lέεo.

  แต่งแล้ว

- No, I'm not married.

  yang mâi dtὲng.

  ยัง ไม่แต่ง

- I'm single.

  pǒm/chán bpen sòot.

  ผม/ฉันเป็นโสด

- I'm divorced.

  pǒm/chán yàa gàp fεεn
    lέεo.

  ผม/ฉันหย่ากับแฟนแล้ว

"Yes" and "No"

Thai has no single word for "yes" or for "no". To answer "yes", you can repeat the relevant word from the question. To answer "no", you say "mâi" followed by the relevant word. For example:

❏ Are you free? wâang mái? (ว่างมั้ย)
   Free. (Yes.) wâang. (ว่าง)
   Not free. (No.) mâi wâang. (ไม่ว่าง)
❏ Is it good? dii mái? (ดีมั้ย)
   Good. (Yes.) dii. (ดี)
   Not good. (No.) mâi dii. (ไม่ดี)

Omitting Pronouns

Many times, the Thai do not use subject pronouns. You have to guess from the context and situation who the speaker is referring to. In this book we omit some subject pronouns, especially first person (I) and second person (you), when they would usually be left out in normal speech.
Example:

(I) don't like it.   mâi chɔ̂ɔp.
                                            ไม่ชอบ

The litteral translation for the above sentence is "don't like" which can mean "I don't like (it)" or "you don't like (it)" depending on the context.

◆   How many children do   (kun) mii lûuk gǐi kon?
    you have?   (คุณ) มีลูกกี่คน?
    ● Two.   sɔ̌ɔng kon.
                                    สองคน

    ● None.   mâi-mii.
                                    ไม่มี

    ● None yet.   yang mâi-mii.
                                    ยังไม่มี

◆   I want to learn Thai from you. yàak rian paa-sǎa tai
                                       gàp kun.
                                    อยากเรียนภาษาไทยกับคุณ

◆   Can you teach me Thai?   sɔ̌ɔn paa-sǎa tai hâi pǒm/
                                    chán nɔ̀i dâai mái?
                                    สอนภาษาไทยให้ผม/ฉันหน่อย
                                       ได้ไหม?

- Yes.   dâai.
                                ได้

- I don't know how to teach.   sɔ̌ɔn mâi-bpen.
                                สอนไม่เป็น

◆ When do you want to start?   yàak rə̂m rian mûa-rài?
                                อยากเริ่มเรียนเมื่อไหร่?

- Now!   dǐao-níi ləəi!
                                เดี๋ยวนี้เลย!

- As soon as possible.   yàak rian reo-reo.
                                อยากเรียนเร็วๆ

◆ What kind of men do you like? (kun) chɔ̂ɔp pûu-chaai
                                    bɛ̀ɛp-nǎi?
                                (คุณ) ชอบผู้ชายแบบไหน?

- I like Caucasian men.   chán chɔ̂ɔp pûu-chaai
                                    fa-ràng.
                                ฉันชอบผู้ชายฝรั่ง

- Older men who are sweet   chɔ̂ɔp kon gɛ̀ɛ tîi nâa-rák
    and kind.   lɛ́ jai-dii.
                                ชอบคนแก่ที่น่ารักและก็ใจดี

- Tall and handsome men.   chɔ̂ɔp kon sǔung
                                    lɛ́-gɔ̂ɔ lɔ̀ɔ.
                                ชอบคนสูงและก็หล่อ

- Rich men.   chɔ̂ɔp kon ruai.
                                ชอบคนรวย

- Romantic men.   chɔ̂ɔp kon roo-mɛɛn-dtìk.
                                ชอบคนโรแมนติก

- Unselfish men.

    chɔ̂ɔp kon ɗi mâi
        hěn-gɛ̀ɛ-dtua.
    ชอบคนที่ไม่เห็นแก่ตัว

◆ What kind of women do
    you like?

    (kun) chɔ̂ɔp pûu-yǐing
        bɛ̀ɛp-nǎi?
    (คุณ) ชอบผู้หญิงแบบไหน?

- I like Asian women.

    pǒm chɔ̂ɔp pûu-yǐng
        ee-chia.
    ผมชอบผู้หญิงเอเซีย

- Young and pretty women.

    pûu-ying sǎao lé sǔai.
    ผู้หญิงสาวและสวย

- Nice, gentle and kind.

    nâa-rák, su-pâap lé jai-dii.
    น่ารัก สุภาพและใจดี

- Intelligent and independent
    woman.

    pûu-ying cha-làat lé chûai
        dtua-eeng dâai.
    ผู้หญิงฉลาดและช่วยตัวเองได้

Who are fa-ràng ?

The generic (and somewhat formal) term for "foreigner" is kon dtàang châat (คนต่างชาติ) or chaao dtàang châat (ชาวต่างชาติ), but people of European ancestory are often called fa-ràng. One theory is that the term comes from the word "France" and later came to mean anyone who looked remotely French. Nowadays, the most accurate translation is probably "Caucasian". That's what we use in this book.

Another generic term, kɛ̀ɛk (แขก), refers to people of Middle Eastern or Indian ancestry. Foreigners are also commonly referred to by their country of origin ("so and so is Japanese, Canadian, Greek", etc.).

◆ I'm not rich, but I'm sincere.　　pŏm/chán mâi ruai,
　　　　　　　　　　　　　　　　　　 dtὲε jing-jai.
　　　　　　　　　　　　　　　　　ผม/ฉันไม่รวย แต่จริงใจ

◆ I like ＿＿＿ people.　　chɔ̂ɔp kon＿＿＿.
　　　　　　　　　　　　　　ชอบคน＿＿＿＿

◆ I like kind people.　　chɔ̂ɔp kon jai dii.
　　　　　　　　　　　　　ชอบคนใจดี

◆ I don't like ＿＿＿ people.　　mâi chɔ̂ɔp kon＿＿＿.
　　　　　　　　　　　　　　　　ไม่ชอบคน＿＿＿＿

◆ I don't like lazy people.　　mâi chɔ̂ɔp kon kîi-gìat.
　　　　　　　　　　　　　　　ไม่ชอบคนขี้เกียจ

◆ You are very ＿＿＿.　　kun ＿＿＿ mâak.
　　　　　　　　　　　　　คุณ. ＿＿＿ มาก

◆ You are very charming.　　kun mii sa-nὲe mâak.
　　　　　　　　　　　　　　คุณมีเสน่ห์มาก

Some adjectives used to describe people:

beautiful	sŭai สวย
big	yài, dtua-dtoo ใหญ่, ตัวโต
brave	glâa กล้า
calm	jai-yen, sù-kŭm ใจเย็น, สุขุม
charming	mii sa-nὲe มีเสน่ห์
cheerful	râa-rəəng ร่าเริง

clean	sa-àat สะอาด
cowardly	kîi klàat ขี้ขลาด
cunning	jâo-lêe เจ้าเล่ห์
cute	nâa-rák น่ารัก
dirty	sòk-ga-bpròk สกปรก
famous	mii chนน-sĭang มีชื่อเสียง
fat	ûan อ้วน
frugal	bpra-yàt ประหยัด
funny	dta-lòk ตลก
hard-working	ka-yăn ขยัน
healthy	sùk-ka-pâap dii สุขภาพดี
intelligent	chà-làat ฉลาด
interesting	nâa-sŏnjai น่าสนใจ
lazy	kîi-gìat ขี้เกียจ
modern	tansa-măi ทันสมัย
neat	rîap-rɔ́ɔi เรียบร้อย
old	gὲɛ แก่
polite	sù-pâap สุภาพ
pretty	sŭai สวย
quiet	ngîap เงียบ
reliable	wái-jai-dâai ไว้ใจได้
sexy	séksîi เซ็กซี่
shy	kîi-aai ขี้อาย
sincere	jing-jai จริงใจ
sloppy	mâi-ao-năi ไม่เอาไหน
small	lék เล็ก
stingy (cheap)	kîi-nĭao ขี้เหนียว
strong	kɛ̆ng-rɛɛng แข็งแรง
stupid	ngôo โง่
thin	pɔ̆ɔm ผอม

trustworthy	chûa-jai-dâai เชื่อใจได้
ugly	nâa-glìat น่าเกลียด
young	aa-yú-nɔ́ɔi อายุน้อย

◆ Where do you live?
bâan kun yùu ʧii-nǎi?
บ้านคุณอยู่ที่ไหน?

● No far from here.
mâi glai jàak ʧii-níi.
ไม่ไกลจากที่นี่

● In Bangkok.
yùu nai grung-têep.
อยู่ในกรุงเทพ

◆ Where are you staying?
kun pák ʧii-nǎi?
คุณพักที่ไหน?

● At the City Hotel.
ʧii roong-rɛɛm si-ʧii.
ที่โรงแรมซิตี้

● With my friend.
pák gàp pûan.
พักกับเพื่อน

◆ I enjoy talking with you.
kui gàp kun sa-nùk mâak.
คุยกับคุณสนุกมาก

◆ Please tell me your address.
kɔ̌ɔ ʧii-yùu kun dûai.
ขอที่อยู่คุณด้วย

◆ Please tell me your phone number.
kɔ̌ɔ bəə-too-ra-sàp kun dûai.
ขอเบอร์โทรศัพท์คุณด้วย

◆ I'll keep in touch.
jà dtìt-dtɔ̀ɔ bpai-hǎa.
จะติดต่อไปหา

◆   I hope to see you again.   wăng-wâa jà dâai jɔɔ-gan
                                        ˈiik.
                                        หวังว่าจะได้เจอกันอีก

◆   I want to see you again.   pǒm/chan yàak jɔɔ kun ˈiik.
                                        ผม / ฉันอยากเจอคุณอีก

◆   Give me a call.   too maa ná.
                                        โทรมาหานะ

◆   I'll give you a call.   jà too bpai hǎa.
                                        จะโทรไปหา

◆   I'll call you tomorrow.   prûng-níi jà too tǔng kun.
                                        พรุ่งนี้จะโทรถึงคุณ

◆   Don't forget.   yàa lɯɯm ná.
                                        อย่าลืมนะ

Names and Pronouns

Thai has numerous pronouns, the use of which depends on one's age, social status and respect for the person being spoken to. Fortunately, as a foreigner, you are not expected to navigate all these social booby traps! The pronouns shown below are probably the only ones you will need.

Virtually all Thai people have nicknames in addition to their official names and, when you know them well, they prefer to be called by their nicknames. Women and girls, in particular, often call themselves by their nicknames instead of using chán or di-chán .

You can find more information about how to use pronouns and nicknames in *Thai for Intermediate Learners.*

Some Common Pronouns

I	*pŏm* (male speakers),
	chán/di-chán (female speakers)
We	*rao, pûak-rao*
You	*kun*
She/He/They	*káo*
It or They	*man* Used for animals and things only. When referring to people it is a derogatory term.
They	*pûak-káo* (people), *pûak-man* (animals or things only)

Asking General Questions in Thai

What's your name?

kun chûu a-rai?
คุณชื่ออะไร?

How old are you?

kun aa-yú tâo-rài?
คุณอายุเท่าไหร่?

Where do you live?

kun yùu tîi-năi?
คุณอยู่ที่ไหน?

I would like to have your address.

kɔ̌ɔ tîi-yùu kun dûai.
ขอที่อยู่คุณด้วย

What's this?

nîi a-rai?
นี่อะไร?

What's it called in Thai?	paa-saa tai rîak-wâa a-rai? ภาษาไทยเรียกว่าอะไร?
Are you married?	kun dtɛ̀ng-ngaan rú-yang? คุณแต่งงานรึยัง?
How many children do you have?	kun mii lûuk gìi kon? คุณมีลูกกี่คน?
Can I call you?	too bpai hăa kun dâai mái? โทรไปหาคุณได้มั้ย?
Have you ever been to _____?	kun kəəi bpai _____ mái? คุณเคยไป _____ มั้ย?
Do you like _____?	kun chɔ̂ɔp _____ mái? คุณชอบ _____ มั้ย?

Note: Don't forget to add the particle kráp (for male speakers) or kâ (for female speakers) at the end of your questions when you want to be more polite.

CHAPTER THREE
Courting

"Whether they yield or refuse, it delights women to have been asked." —OVID, *Ars Amatoria*

◆ Do you have a boyfriend/ girlfriend?

kun mii fɛɛn rú-yang?

คุณมีแฟนรึยัง?

• Not yet.

yang mâi-mii.

ยังไม่มี

• Yes, I do.

mii lɛ́ɛo.

มีแล้ว

• I'm single.

pŏm/chán yang bpen sòot.

ผม/ฉันยังเป็นโสด

◆ What are you doing tonight?

kɯɯn níi kun tam a-rai?

คืนนี้คุณทำอะไร?

- I don't know yet .

yang mâi rúu-wâa jà tam
   a-rai.
ยังไม่รู้ว่าจะทำอะไร

- Nothing special.

mâi mii a-rai pí-sèet.
ไม่มีอะไรพิเศษ

- I think I want to go out.

kít-wâa jà ɔ̀ɔk bpai
   kâang-nɔ̂ɔk.
คิดว่าจะออกไปข้างนอก

- I think I will watch T.V.

kít-wâa jà duu tii-wii.
คิดว่าจะดูทีวี

◆ Are you free tonight?

kɯɯn-níi kun wâang mái?
คืนนี้คุณว่างไหม?

- Yes. Why do you ask?

wâang. tăam tammai?
ว่างถามทำไม

- No, I have to work tonight.

mâi wâang. kɯɯn-níi
   dtɔ̂ng tam-ngaan.
ไม่ว่าง คืนนี้ต้องทำงาน

- Sorry, I already have a date.

kɔ̌ɔ-tôot. mii nát lɛ́ɛo.
ขอโทษด้วย มีนัดแล้ว

◆ Are you free next Friday night?

wan sùk nâa, kun wâang
   mai?
วันศุกร์หน้าคุณว่างไหม?

- Maybe.

àat-jà wâang.
อาจจะว่าง

- I'm not sure.

mâi nɛ̂ɛ-jai.
ไม่แน่ใจ

- I have to check.

dtɔ̂ng chék duu gɔ̀ɔn.
ต้องเช็คดูก่อน

◆ Can I see you tomorrow?

    prûng-níi jəə dâai r

    พรุ่งนี้เจอได้ไหม?

  ● I think so.

    kít-wâa dâai.

    คิดว่าได้

  ● Yes, I'm free tomoorow.

    dâai, prûng-níi wâang.

    ได้ พรุ่งนี้ว่าง

  ● I have things to do
    tomorrow.

    prûng-níi mii tu-rá.

    พรุ่งนี้มีธุระ

◆ Maybe some other time.

    ao-wái oo-gàat nâa.

    เอาไว้โอกาสหน้า

◆ Do you want to have dinner?
    with me tonight?

    kɯɯnníi bpai taan kâao-yen
    gàp pŏm/chán mái?

    คืนนี้ไปทานข้าวเย็นกับผม/ฉันมั้ย?

  ● O.K.

    oo-kee.

    โอเค

  ● Sorry, I can't make it
    tonight.

    kɔ̌ɔ-tôot ná. kɯɯnníi bpai
    mâi-dâai.

    ขอโทษนะ คืนนี้ไปไม่ได้

◆ I'd like to invite you to dinner.

    yàak chəən kun bpai taan
    kâao-yen dûai.

    อยากเชิญคุณไปทานข้าวเย็นด้วย

◆ Thank you for inviting me.

    kɔ̀ɔp-kun tîi chəən.

    ขอบคุณที่เชิญ

◆ Thank you for calling.

    kɔ̀ɔpkun tîi too maa.

    ขอบคุณที่โทรมา

Chaperons

So you have a date. Congratulations! Don't be surprised, however, if things turn out a bit more crowded than you expected. Even mature Thai women will likely want to bring a friend or relative with them on the first few dates. Take this into account when you suggest activities. Chaperons serve several purposes. They assure the well being and virtue of your date and protect her reputation. A Thai woman alone with an unfamiliar foreigner may be mistaken for a prostitute. There are also benefits for the chaperon. Thai dates almost always involve food--enough in itself to motivate a younger brother or sister to come along. Add in the opportunity to eavesdrop on an older sister and exotic foreigner and the temptation becomes irresistible! All of the above refers to Thai women. Thai men are not likely to insist on a chaperon.

◆ I've never dated a Thai girl before.

pŏm mâi kəəi mii nát gàp pûu-yĭng tai.
ผมไม่เคยมีนัดกับผู้หญิงไทย

◆ I've never dated a Thai man before.

chán mâi kəəi mii nát gàp pûu-chaai tai.
ฉันไม่เคยมีนัดกับผู้ชายไทย

◆ I've never had an Asian girlfriend.

pŏm mâi kəəi mii fɛɛn kon ee-chia.
ผมไม่เคยมีแฟนคนเอเชีย

◆ I've never had a Caucasian boyfriend.

chán mâi kəəi mii fɛɛn fa-ràng.
ฉันไม่เคยมีแฟนฝรั่ง

◆ I just broke up with my
boyfriend/girlfriend.

pŏm/chán pôŋ lâak gàp
fɛɛn.

ผม/ฉันเพิ่งเลิกกับแฟน

◆ I'm looking for somebody.

yàak jà hăa krai sàk kon.

อยากจะหาใครสักคน

◆ I want to find somebody who
understands me.

yàak jà hăa kon fii rúu jai.

อยากจะหาคนที่รู้ใจ

◆ I like your personality.

pŏm/chán chɔ̂ɔp ni-săi kun.

ผม/ฉันชอบนิสัยคุณ

◆ You are such a pretty and
nice girl.

kun bpen pûu-ying fii sŭai
lé nâa-rák.

คุณเป็นผู้หญิงที่สวยและน่ารัก

◆ You are such a handsome
and kind man.

kun bpen pûu-chaai fii lɔ̀ɔ
lé jai-dii.

คุณเป็นผู้ชายที่หล่อและใจดี

◆ You are such a flirt!

kun jâo-chúu jang!

คุณเจ้าชู้จัง!

◆ Your words are so sweet.

kun bpàak wăan jang.

คุณปากหวานจัง

◆ Is that true?

jing rɔ̌ə?

จริงเหรอ?

◆ Are you having a good time?   sa-nùk mái?
                                  สนุกมั้ย?

• Very much.   sa-nùk mâak.
                                  สนุกมาก

• I couldn't have a better time. sa-nùk ɗii-sùt.
                                  สนุกที่สุด

◆ I enjoyed tonight very much.   kɯɯnníi sa-nùk mâak.
                                  คืนนี้สนุกมาก

◆ I always enjoy meeting you.   jəə gàp kun sa-nùk túk
                                     kráng.
                                  เจอกับคุณสนุกทุกครั้ง

◆ Could I hold your hand?   kɔ̌ɔ jàp mɯɯ nɔ̀i dâai mái?
                                  ขอจับมือคุณได้มั้ย?

◆ I want to hold your hand.   yàak jàp mɯɯ kun.
                                  อยากจับมือคุณ

◆ I want to give you a hug.   yàak gɔ̀ɔt kun.
                                  อยากกอดคุณ

◆ Be with me tonight.   kɯɯnníi yùu gàp pǒm/chán
                                     ná.
                                  คืนนี้อยู่กับผม/ฉันนะ

◆ I think it's too fast.   kít-wâa yang reo bpai.
                                  คิดว่ายังเร็วไป

◆   I don't know you well enough.   pǒm/chán yang mâi rúu-jàk
                                          kun dii pɔɔ.
                                      ฉันยังไม่รู้จักคุณดีพอ

◆   I want to wait for a while.   yàak jà rɔɔ-duu gɔ̀ɔn.
                                      อยากจะรอดูก่อน

◆   Give me some more time.   kɔ̌ɔ wee-laa ʔiik nɔ̀i.
                                      ขอเวลาอีกหน่อย

◆   I never thought I would meet   mâi kít-wâa jà dâai jəə
    a person like you here.   kon bɛ̀ɛp kun ʈii-nîi.
                                      ไม่คิดว่าจะได้เจอคนแบบคุณที่นี่

◆   I will think about you.   pǒm/chán jà kíttʉ̌ng kun.
                                      ผม/ฉันจะคิดถึงคุณ

◆   I will dream about you tonight.   kʉʉnníi jà fǎn tʉ̌ng kun.
                                      คืนนี้จะฝันถึงคุณ

◆   When can I see you again?   jà dâai jəə kun ʔiik mʉ̂a-rài?
                                      จะได้เจอคุณอีกเมื่อไหร่?

◆   What about this weekend?   sǎo aa-tít níi bpen ngai?
                                      เสาร์-อาทิตย์นี้เป็นไง?

   ●   You bet.   dâai ləəi.
                                      ได้เลย

   ●   Saturday I work, but Sunday   wan sǎo tam-ngaan, dtɛ̀ɛ
       is fine.   wan aa-tít wâang.
                                      วันเสาร์ทำงาน แต่วันอาทิตย์ว่าง

◆ I can't wait to see you again.   yàak jɔɔ kun reo-reo.

                                        อยากจะเจอคุณเร็วๆ

● Same here.   chên-gan.

                                        เช่นกัน

Sample Situation

In the following situation a male foreigner (John) is dating a Thai woman (Lek). For a foreign female dating a Thai man, the same sample conversations would apply— just change the pronouns (pŏm and chán) and ending particles (kráp or ká/kâ).

At a Thai Restaurant

John is having dinner with Lek at a Thai restaurant in Bangkok. When you are at a Thai restaurant, your Thai date will probably offer to order for you and will likely ask whether you can eat spicy food or not. Thai people usually assume that foreigners, especially Caucasians, cannot eat spicy food. If you do like spicy foods, let your date know. Otherwise, don't worry. There are lots of mild Thai foods for you.

You can find a list of common Thai foods and desserts in the appendix.

Sample Conversation

Lek: kun jɔɔn chɔ̂ɔp aa-hǎan tai mái ká ?

เล็ก   คุณจอห์นชอบอาหารไทยมั้ยคะ?

        Do you like Thai food, John?

John: chɔ̂ɔp mâak kráp. pŏm chɔ̂ɔp aa-hǎan pèt.

จอห์น   ชอบมากครับ ผมชอบอาหารเผ็ด

        Very much. I like spicy food.

Lek: wanníi kun yàak taan a-rai ká?

เล็ก วันนี้คุณอยากทานอะไรคะ?

What would you like to have today?

John: a-rai gɔ̂ɔ dâai kráp. sàng hâi pǒm dûai.

จอห์น อะไรก็ได้ครับ สั่งให้ผมด้วย

I can have anything. Please order for me.

Lek: yàak lɔɔng dtôm-yam-gûng mái ká?

เล็ก อยากลองต้มยำกุ้งมั้ยคะ?

Would you like to try hot & spicy shrimp soup?

John: oo-kee kráp.

จอห์น โอเคครับ

O.K.

Lek: kun kəəi taan som-dtam mái ká?

เล็ก คุณเคยทานส้มตำมั้ยคะ?

Have you ever eaten papaya salad?

John: mâi kəəi kráp, dtὲɛ pǒm rúu wâa kon tai chɔ̂ɔp mâak.

จอห์น ไม่เคยครับ แต่ผมรู้ว่าคนไทยชอบมาก

I've never tried it, but I know that Thai people really like it.

Lek: kun jà dὺɯm a-rai ká?

เล็ก คุณจะดื่มอะไรคะ?

What will you drink?

John: bia tai kráp. pǒm chɔ̂ɔp bia dtraa sǐng.

จอห์น เบียร์ไทยครับ ผมชอบเบียร์ตราสิงห์

Thai beer. I like Singha beer.

Lek: kun yàak taan kɔ̌ɔng-wǎan dûai mái ká?

เล็ก คุณอยากทานของหวานด้วยมั้ยคะ?

Would you like to have dessert?

John: mâi kráp. pǒm ìm lέɛo.

จอห์น ไม่ครับ ผมอิ่มแล้ว

No. I'm already full.

Food Words

beer	bia เบียร์
beef	nûa, nûa-wua เนื้อ, เนื้อวัว
boil/boiled	dtôm ต้ม
breakfast	aa-hǎan cháao อาหารเช้า
chicken	gài ไก่
coffee	gaa-fɛɛ กาแฟ
crab	bpuu ปู
curry	gɛɛng-pèt แกงเผ็ด
dessert	kɔ̌ɔng-wâan ของหวาน
delicious	a-rɔ̀i อร่อย
dinner	aa-hǎan yen อาหารเย็น
duck	bpèt เป็ด
eat (informal)	gin กิน
eat (formal)	taan ทาน
egg	kài ไข่
fish	bplaa ปลา
food	aa-hǎan อาหาร
fry/fried	tɔ̂ɔt ทอด
fruit	pǒn-la-máai ผลไม้
grill/grilled	yâang ย่าง
like	chɔ̂ɔp ชอบ
lunch	aa-hǎan tiang อาหารเที่ยง
ice	náam-kɛ̌ng น้ำแข็ง
noodles	ba-mǐi บะหมี่, (egg noodles)
	guǎi-tǐao ก๋วยเตี๋ยว (rice noodles)
orange juice	náam sôm น้ำส้ม
pork	mǔu หมู
porridge	kâao-dtôm ข้าวต้ม

rice	kâao ข้าว
seafood	aa-hăan ta-lee อาหารทะเล
shrimp	gûng กุ้ง
snack	ka-nŏm ขนม
soup	súp, gɛɛng ซุป, แกง
squid	bplaa-mùk ปลาหมึก
sticky rice	kâao-nĭao ข้าวเหนียว
steam (v.)	nûng นึ่ง
tea	chaa ชา
Thai food	aa-hăan tai อาหารไทย
turkey	gài-nguang ไก่งวง
vegetable	pàk ผัก
vegetarian	gin-jee กินเจ
water	náam น้ำ
whisky	lâo เหล้า
wine	waai ไวน์

Useful Phrases at Restaurants

I want to order _____.

pŏm/chán yàak sàng _____.
ผม/ฉันอยากสั่ง _____

What do you like to eat?

kun chɔ̂ɔp taan a-rai?
คุณชอบทานอะไร?

What would you like to drink?

kun yàak dùum a-rai?
คุณอยากดื่มอะไร?

I'd like a bottle of beer.

kɔ̆ɔ bia nùng kùat.
ขอเบียร์หนึ่งขวด

I'd like a glass of water.	kɔ̌ɔ náam nùng gɛ́ɛo. ขอน้ำหนึ่งแก้ว
I'd like one serving of fried rice.	kɔ̌ɔ kâao-pàt nùng tîi. ขอข้าวผัดหนึ่งที่
I'd like some ice.	kɔ̌ɔ náam kěng dûai. ขอน้ำแข็งด้วย
Is it hot (spicy)?	pèt mái? เผ็ดมั้ย?
This is too hot (spicy).	pèt gɔɔn bpai. เผ็ดเกินไป
This is not hot (spicy).	nîi mâi pèt. นี่ไม่เผ็ด
Is it delicious?	a-rɔ̀i mái? อร่อยมั้ย?
It's delicious.	a-rɔ̀i. อร่อย
It's not delicious.	mâi a-rɔ̀i. ไม่อร่อย
The food is very delicious.	aa-hǎan a-rɔ̀i mâak. อาหารอร่อยมาก

I like Thai food.

pŏm/chán chɔ̂ɔp aa-hǎan
    tai.
ผม/ฉันชอบอาหารไทย

I want some dessert.

yàak taan kɔ̌ɔng-wǎan.
อยากทานของหวาน

I'm already full.

ìm lέεo.
อิ่มแล้ว

That's enough.

pɔɔ lέεo.
พอแล้ว

I'm drunk.

pŏm/chán mao.
ผม/ฉันเมา

Please give me the bill.

gèp ngən dûai.
เก็บเงินด้วย

The food is not expensive.

aa-hǎan mâi pεεng.
อาหารไม่แพง

Do I need to leave a tip?

dtɔ̂ng típ rɯ́ bplàao?
ต้องทิปรึเปล่า?

Expressing Basic Needs or Feelings

I'm hungry.

hǐu kâao.
หิวข้าว

I'm thirsty.   hĭu náam.
                                                หิวน้ำ

I'm tired.   nὺai.
                                                เหนื่อย

I'm exhausted.   nὺai mâak.
                                                เหนื่อยมาก

I'm sleepy.   ngûang-nɔɔn.
                                                ง่วงนอน

I'm excited.   dtὺɯn-dtên.
                                                ตื่นเต้น

I'm hot.   rɔ́ɔn.
                                                ร้อน

I'm cold.   năao.
                                                หนาว

I feel sick.   mâi sa-baai.
                                                ไม่สบาย

I have a headache.   bpùat hŭa.
                                                ปวดหัว

I have a stomachache.   bpùat tɔ́ɔng.
                                                ปวดท้อง

I have diarrhea.

tɔ́ɔng sǐa.
ท้องเสีย

I have jet-lag.

bpràp wee-laa mâi tan.
ปรับเวลาไม่ทัน

I need some medicine.

dtɔ̂ng-gaan yaa.
ต้องการยา

I need some rest.

dtɔ̂ng-gaan pákpɔ̀n.
ต้องการพักผ่อน

I want to see a doctor.

yàak bpai-hǎa mɔ̌ɔ.
อยากไปหาหมอ

I need help.

dtɔ̂ɔng-gaan kwaam
    chûai-lǔa.
ต้องการความช่วยเหลือ

Come here.

maa-nîi.
มานี่

Help!

chûai-dûai.
ช่วยด้วย

Watch out!

ra-wang!
ระวัง !

I want to drink some water.

yàak gin/dùum náam.
อยากกิน/ดื่มน้ำ

I want to have a cup of coffee.   yàak gin/dùum gaa-fɛɛ.
                                               อยากกิน/ดื่มกาแฟ

I want to buy some <u>cigarettes</u>.   yàak súu <u>bu-rǐi</u>.
                                               อยากซื้อ<u>บุหรี่</u>

I want to buy some <u>medicine</u>.   yàak súu <u>yaa</u>.
                                               อยากซื้อ<u>ยา</u>

I have to use the restroom.   jà bpai hɔ̂ng-náam.
                                               จะไปห้องน้ำ

Where is the restroom?   hɔ̂ng-náam yùu tîi-nǎi?
                                               ห้องน้ำอยู่ที่ไหน?

It is too loud.   sǐang dang gəən bpai.
                                               เสียงดังเกินไป

Can you turn down the   lót ɛɛ long dâai mái?
   air-conditioner?   ลดแอร์ลงได้มั้ย?

Can you turn up the air-conditioner.   bpə̀ət ɛɛ kûn ǐik dâai mai?
                                               เปิดแอร์ขึ้นอีกได้มั้ย?

Turn on the fan.   bpə̀ət pátlom dûai.
                                               เปิดพัดลมด้วย

It's very hot and stuffy in here.   tîi-nîi rɔ́ɔn lé àp mâak.
                                               ที่นี่ร้อนและอับมาก

Can I use the telephone?	kɔ̌ɔ châi too-ra-sàp dâai mái? ขอใช้โทรศัพท์ได้มั้ย
Can I have more water?	kɔ̌ɔ náam ìik dâai mái? ขอน้ำอีกได้มั้ย?
I'm lost.	lǒng taang. หลงทาง
How do I go to_____?	bpai _____ yang-ngai? ไป _____ ยังไง
Hello (on the phone).	han-lǒo. ฮัลโหล
I would like to speak (on the phone) with ____.	kɔ̌ɔ sǎai gàp ____. ขอสายกับ ____
I need more money.	dtɔ̂ɔng-gaan ngən ìik. ต้องการเงินอีก
I need to go to the bank.	dtɔ̂ng bpai ta-naa-kaan. ต้องไปธนาคาร
I need to exchange money	dtɔ̂ng-gaan lɛ̂ɛk ngən. ต้องการแลกเงิน
I need to call a taxi.	jà rîak rót téksîi. จะเรียกรถแท็กซี่

I want to go home.	yàak glàp bâan. อยากกลับบ้าน
I want to _____ (verb).	yàak _____. อยาก _____
I want _____ (noun).	yàak dâai _____. อยากได้ _____
I have a question.	mii kamtăam. มีคำถาม
I have to leave.	dtɔ̂ng rîip bpai. ต้องรีบไป
I have to go back to my hotel.	dtɔ̂ng glàp roong-rɛɛm. ต้องกลับโรงแรม
I'm leaving tomorrow.	jà glàp prûng-níi. จะกลับพรุ่งนี้
I'm going back to my country.	jà glàp bprà-têet. จะกลับประเทศ
I understand.	kâo-jai. เข้าใจ
I don't understand.	mâi kâo-jai. ไม่เข้าใจ

I don't know.

mâi rúu.
ไม่รู้

I think so, too.

kít mǔan-gan.
คิดเหมือนกัน

I don't think so.

mâi kít yàang nán.
ไม่คิดอย่างนั้น

I believe (you).

chûa.
เชื่อ

I don't believe (you).

mâi chûa.
ไม่เชื่อ

I'm not sure.

mâi nêɛ-jai.
ไม่แน่ใจ

I'm kidding.

pûut lên.
พูดเล่น

I like it.

chɔ̂ɔp.
ชอบ

I like it very much.

chɔ̂ɔp mâak.
ชอบมาก

I don't like it.

mâi chɔ̂ɔp.
ไม่ชอบ

I forgot.	lʉʉm. ลืม
I remember.	jam dâai. จำได้
I don't remember.	jam mâi dâai. จำไม่ได้
Is that right?	tùuk mái? ถูกมั้ย?
No problem.	mai mii bpan-hǎa. ไม่มีปัญหา
That's interesting.	nâa-sonjai. น่าสนใจ
Let's go.	bpai gan tɔ̀. ไปกันเถอะ
Are you ready?	sèt rʉ́ yang? เสร็จรึยัง?
May I smoke?	sùup bu-rìi dâai mái? สูบบุหรี่ได้มั้ย?
No smoking.	hâam sùup bu-rìi. ห้ามสูบบุหรี่

I'm ready.	sèt léɛo. เสร็จแล้ว
I'm not ready.	yang mâi sèt. ยังไม่เสร็จ
I'm busy.	yûng mâak. ยุ่งมาก
I'm happy.	mii kwaamsùk. มีความสุข
I'm enjoying myself.	sa-nùk mâak. สนุกมาก
I'm sad.	rú-sùk sâo-jai. รู้สึกเศร้าใจ
I'm fine.	sa-baai dii. สบายดี
I'm angry.	pǒm/chán gròot. ผม/ฉันโกรธ
I'm mad at you.	pǒm/chán gròot kun. ผม/ฉันโกรธคุณ
I'm lonely.	pǒm/chán rúu-sùk ngǎo. ผม/ฉันรู้สึกเหงา

I'm surprised.	pŏm/chán rúu-sùk bprà-làat jai. ผม/ฉันรู้สึกประหลาดใจ
I'm disappointed.	pŏm/chán rúu-sùk pìtwăng. ผม/ฉันรู้สึกผิดหวัง
I'm worried.	pŏm/chán rúu-sùk gangwon. ผม/ฉันรู้สึกกังวล
I'm confused.	pŏm/chán rúu-sùk sàpsŏn. ผม/ฉันรู้สึกสับสน
I'm hurt (emotionally).	pŏm/chán rúu-sùk jèp hŭa-jai. ผม/ฉันรู้สึกเจ็บหัวใจ
I'm embarrassed.	pŏm/chán rúu-sùk aai. ผม/ฉันรู้สึกอาย
I'm desperate.	pŏm/chán rúu-sùk mòtwăng. ผม/ฉันรู้สึกหมดหวัง
I envy you.	pŏm/chán ĭtchăa kun. ผม/ฉันอิจฉาคุณ
I have a broken heart.	pŏm/chán òkhàk. ผม/ฉันอกหัก
I don't want to impose.	greeng-jai. เกรงใจ

It's boring.

nâa-bùa.
น่าเบื่อ

I feel homesick.

kít-tŭng bâan.
คิดถึงบ้าน

I made a mistake.

tam pìt plâat.
ทำผิดพลาด

I agree with you.

pŏm/chán hĕn dûai.
ผม/ฉันเห็นด้วย

I don't agree with you.

pŏm/chán mâi hĕn dûai.
ผม/ฉันไม่เห็นด้วย

Listen!

fang.
ฟัง

Look!

duu sǐ.
ดูสิ

A little bit.

nít nɔ̀i.
นิดหน่อย

Very. A lot.

mâak.
มาก

Speak more slowly.

pûut cháa-cháa.
พูดช้าๆ

Speak up!   pûut dang-dang!
                                 พูดดังๆ !

Say it again.   pûut ìik kráng.
                                 พูดอีกครั้ง

I can't hear.   mâi dâi-yin.
                                 ไม่ได้ยิน

Wait a minute.   rɔɔ-dǐao/rɔɔ-sàk-krûu.
                                 รอเดี๋ยว/รอสักครู่

It's too loud.   sǐang dang gəən bpai.
                                 เสียงดังเกินไป

Who Pays?

Since dates often turn into group affairs, the question of who should pay comes up. The answer is, "probably you"— for everybody. Going "Dutch", with each person paying his or her own share of the expenses, is not a Thai custom. To offer to pay only part of a bill or to reimburse someone for your share would be considered stingy and very tacky.

In a dating situation the man usually pays for everything. In general social situations between equals the person who invites usually pays. When there is no clear host, the person with the highest status will generally ask for the bill. Sometimes none of these situations really fit, so someone (hopefully you) steps up and treats everybody. Be consoled by the fact that, although it may be hard on your pocket book, all this is having a healthy effect on your social status. If, in spite of your best efforts, someone else pays the bill, accept it gracefully and try to reciprocate at a later time.

CHAPTER FOUR
Romantic Conversation

"Love and a cough cannot be hid." —GEORGE HERBERT, *Jacula Prudentum*

◆ I love you.

pŏm/chán rák kun.
ผม/ฉันรักคุณ

◆ I really love you.

rák kun jing-jing.
รักคุณจริงๆ

◆ I love you with all my heart.

rák kun mòt hǔa-jai.
รักคุณหมดหัวใจ

◆ I miss you.   pŏm/chán kít-tŭng kun.
                                      ผม/ฉันคิดถึงคุณ

◆ I feel so lonely.   pŏm/chán ngăo mâak.
                                      ผม/ฉันเหงามาก

◆ I'm so lonely without you.   mâi mii kun, ngăo mâak.
                                      ไม่มีคุณ เหงามาก

◆ I don't want to be here   mâi yàak yùu tîi-nîi tâa
       without you.   mâi mii kun.
                                      ไม่อยากอยู่ที่นี่ถ้าไม่มีคุณ

◆ Can you be my boy/girlfriend? bpen fɛɛn pŏm/chán
                                      dâai mái?
                                      เป็นแฟนผม/ฉันได้มั้ย?

◆ I am single.   pŏm/chán bpen sòot.
                                      ผม/ฉันเป็นโสด

◆ I don't have anyone in my   mâi mii krai yùu nai hŭa-jai.
       heart.   ไม่มีใครอยู่ในหัวใจ

◆ I want to be with you.   yàak yùu gàp kun.
                                      อยากอยู่กับคุณ

◆ I want to be with you all   yàak yùu gàp kun
       the time.   dta-lòot wee-laa.
                                      อยากอยู่กับคุณตลอดเวลา

◆   I want to be with you forever.   yàak yùu gàp kun
                                              dta-lɔ̀ɔt bpai.
                                         อยากอยู่กับคุณตลอดไป

◆   Why do you love me?   tammai kun tʉ̌ng rák
                                         pǒm/chán?
                                         ทำไมคุณถึงรักผม/ฉัน?

●   Because you are _____.   prɔ́-wâa kun _____.
                                         เพราะว่าคุณ _____

    calm   jai-yen   ใจเย็น
    intelligent   cha-làat   ฉลาด
    kind   jai-dii   ใจดี
    nice   nâa-rák   น่ารัก
    polite   su-pâap   สุภาพ
    rich   ruai   รวย

◆   I can't forget you.   lʉʉm kun mâi-dâai.
                                         ลืมคุณไม่ได้

◆   I dream about you all the time.   fǎn tʉ̌ng kun dta-lɔ̀ɔt
                                              wee-laa.
                                         ฝันถึงคุณตลอดเวลา

◆   I will dream about you every   jà fǎn tʉ̌ng kun túk kʉʉn.
    night.   จะฝันถึงคุณทุกคืน

◆   I will dream about you tonight.   kʉʉn níi jà fǎn tʉ̌ng kun.
                                         คืนนี้จะฝันถึงคุณ

◆ I dreamt about you last night.

mûa-kuun făn tŭng kun.
เมื่อคืนฝันถึงคุณ

◆ You're the woman of my dreams.

kun kuu pûu-yĭng nai făn.
คุณคือผู้หญิงในฝัน

◆ You're the man of my dreams.

kun kuu pûu-chaai nai făn.
คุณคือผู้ชายในฝัน

◆ I want to know all about you.

yàak rúu rûang kŏong kun.
อยากรู้เรื่องของคุณ

◆ This is my first love.

nîi bpen rák rêɛk kŏong
pŏm/chán.
นี่เป็นรักแรกของผม/ฉัน

◆ You are very beautiful.

kun sŭai mâak.
คุณสวยมาก

◆ You are very charming.

kun mii sa-nèe mâak.
คุณมีเสน่ห์มาก

◆ You are very handsome.

kun lɔ̀ɔ mâak.
คุณหล่อมาก

◆ You are very cute.

kun nâa-rák mâak.
คุณน่ารักมาก

◆ You have beautiful eyes.

dtaa kun sŭai mâak.
ตาคุณสวยมาก

◆ You have a cute nose.

ja-mùuk kɔ̌ɔng kun
    nâa-rák.
จมูกของคุณน่ารัก

◆ I like your smile.

pǒm/chán chɔ̂ɔp yím
kɔ̌ɔng kun.
ผม/ฉันชอบยิ้มของคุณ

◆ I like your outfit.

pǒm/chán chɔ̂ɔp chút tîi
    kun sài.
ผม/ฉันชอบชุดที่คุณใส่

◆ I like looking at you.

pǒm/chán chɔ̂ɔp mɔɔng
    kun.
ผม/ฉันชอบมองคุณ

◆ I want to share my life
    with you.

yàak cháai chii-wít gàp
    kun.
อยากใช้ชีวิตกับคุณ

◆ Love at first sight.

rák rɛ̂ɛk póp.
รักแรกพบ

◆ I've never met a man like you.

mâi kəəi jəə pûu-chaai
    yàang kun.
ไม่เคยเจอผู้ชายอย่างคุณ

◆ I've never met a woman
    like you.

mâi kəəi jəə pûu-yǐng
    yàang kun.
ไม่เคยเจอผู้หญิงอย่างคุณ

◆ I've never loved anybody like   mâi kəəi rák krai bpὲɛp
   this before.   níi maa gɔ̀ɔn.
                                         ไม่เคยรักใครแบบนี้มาก่อน

◆ I'm serious about you.   pŏm/chán jing-jai gàp kun.
                                         ผม/ฉันจริงใจกับคุณ

◆ I'm crazy about you.   pŏm/chán klâng-klái kun.
                                         ผม/ฉันคลั่งไคล้คุณ

◆ I love you, not your money.   pŏm/chán rák kun,
                                         mâi-châi ngən kɔ̌ɔng kun.
                                         ผม/ฉันรักคุณ ไม่ใช่เงินของคุณ

◆ I don't care how much money   pŏm/chán mâi-sŏn rɔ̀k wâa
   you have.   kun mii ngən tâo-rài.
                                         ผม/ฉันไม่สนใจหรอกว่าคุณมีเงิน
                                         เท่าไหร่

◆ I'm so happy being around   mii kwaam sùk tîi yùu
   you.   glâi kun.
                                         มีความสุขที่อยู่ใกล้คุณ

◆ Are you really serious   kun jing-jai gàp pŏm/chán
   about me?   jing rʉ́ bplàao?
                                         คุณจริงใจกับผม/ฉันจริงรึเปล่า?

   ● Really.   jing-jing.
                                         จริงๆ

   ● Yes, I'm serious and sincere.   tâng jing-jang lέ jing-jai.
                                         ทั้งจริงจังและจริงใจ

- I like you as a friend. — chɔ̂ɔp kun bɛ̀ɛp pɨ̂an.
  ชอบคุณแบบเพื่อน

- I don't know yet. — yang mâi rúu.
  ยังไม่รู้

◆ My heart is all yours. — hǔa-jai pǒm/chán bpen
  kɔ̌ɔng kun.
  หัวใจผม/ฉันเป็นของคุณ

◆ You mean everything to me. — kun kɨɨ túk-sǐng túk-yàang
  samràp pǒm/chán.
  คุณคือทุกสิ่งทุกอย่างสำหรับผม/ฉัน

◆ You are my precious thing. — kun bpen sǐng mii kâa
  kɔ̌ɔng pǒm/chán.
  คุณเป็นสิ่งมีค่าของผม/ฉัน

◆ I love you only. — pǒm/chán rák kun kon
  diao.
  ผม/ฉันรักคุณคนเดียว

◆ I'm so happy being around you. — mii kwaam-sùk mâak tîi
  dâai yùu glâi kun.
  มีความสุขมากที่ได้อยู่ใกล้คุณ

◆ I will always love you. — pǒm/chán jà rák kun
  dtá-lɔ̀ɔt bpai.
  ผม/ฉันจะรักคุณตลอดไป

◆   I can't love anyone else.   pŏm/chán rák krai mâi
                                              dâai ǐik lɛ́ɛo.
                                         ผม/ฉันรักใครไม่ได้อีกแล้ว

◆   I can't wait to see you again.   pŏm/chán yàak jɔɔ kun
                                              reo-reo.
                                         ผม/ฉันอยากจะเจอคุณเร็วๆ

◆   I want to see you as soon as   pŏm/chán yàak jɔɔ kun
     possible.   hâi reo ɕii-sùt.
                                         ผม/ฉันอยากเจอคุณให้เร็วที่สุด

◆   I don't want to leave you.   pŏm/chán mâi yàak bpai
                                              jàak kun.
                                         ผม/ฉันไม่อยากไปจากคุณ

◆   I don't want you to leave.   pŏm/chán mâi yàak
                                              hâi kun bpai.
                                         ผม/ฉันไม่อยากให้คุณไป

◆   You can trust me.   kɔ̌ɔ hâi chûa-jai pŏm/chán.
                                         ขอให้เชื่อใจผม/ฉัน

◆   I will be faithful to you.   pŏm/chán jà sɨ̂ɨ-sàt dtɔ̀ɔ
                                              kun.
                                         ผม/ฉันจะซื่อสัตย์ต่อคุณ

◆   You're my best friend.   kun bpen pɨ̂an ɕii dii ɕii-sùt
                                              kɔɔng pŏm/chán.
                                         คุณเป็นเพื่อนที่ดีที่สุดของผม/ฉัน

◆ I will never cheat on you. pǒm/chán jà mâi nɔ̂ɔk-jai
                              kun.
                              ผม/ฉันจะไม่นอกใจคุณ

◆ I still remember the moment yang jam-dâai dtɔɔn tîi rao
   we met.   jəə gan.
                              ยังจำได้ตอนที่เราเจอกัน

◆ I will call you every night. jà too bpai hǎa túk kʉʉn.
                              จะโทรไปหาทุกคืน

◆ I had a good time with you. yùu gàp kun sa-nùk mâak.
                              อยู่กับคุณสนุกมาก

◆ I will miss you.   pǒm/chán jà kít-tʉ̌ng kun.
                              ผม/ฉันจะคิดถึงคุณ

◆ I have fallen in love with you. rák kun kâo lɛ́ɛo.
                              รักคุณเข้าแล้ว

◆ I love you with all my heart. rák kun mòt hǔa-jai.
                              รักคุณหมดหัวใจ

◆ I'm yours.   pǒm/chán bpen kɔ̌ɔng kun.
                              ผม/ฉันเป็นของคุณ

◆ You're mine.   kun bpen kɔ̌ɔng pǒm/chán.
                              คุณเป็นของผม/ฉัน

◆ You are so romantic.   kun roo-mɛɛn-dtìk mâak.
                                        คุณโรแมนติกมาก

◆ It's hard to say how I feel.   yâak tîi jà bɔ̀ɔk kwaam
                                            rúu-sùk.
                                        ยากที่จะบอกความรู้สึก

◆ Think about me sometimes.   kít tʉ̌ng pǒm/chán bâang .
                                        คิดถึงผม/ฉันบ้าง

◆ I don't want to sleep alone.   mâi yàak nɔɔn kon diao.
                                        ไม่อยากนอนคนเดียว

◆ You are my sweetheart.   kun kʉʉ sùt tîi-rák kɔɔng
                                            pǒm/chán.
                                        คุณคือสุดที่รักของผม/ฉัน

◆ Don't forget me.   yàa lʉʉm pǒm/chán.
                                        อย่าลืมผม/ฉัน

◆ Honey.   tîi-rák.
                                        ที่รัก

◆ My dearest.   sùt tîi-rák.
                                        สุดที่รัก

◆ Sweetheart.   wǎanjai
                                        หวานใจ

Showing Affection in Public

These days, young Thai lovers can often be seen holding hands or hugging each other in public— much to the embarassment and consternation of their elders! Traditionally, it is socially taboo for lovers or even married couples to show affection in public. This goes not only for kissing and snuggling but virtually any physical contact. For example, most Thai women don't like to be seen holding hands with men in public, especially with foreign men. One reason for this is that they don't want to lose face and have people think that they are prostitutes— even when they are. Be especially sensitive to these concerns when you are around her family and friends. The country girl may not mind holding hands in a Bangkok shopping mall but will want to be strictly proper while visiting her home village. Just because she wants to be a "polite" girl doesn't mean she won't be an affectionate lover when she is alone with you. While the above comments apply to both men and women, the double standard is alive and well in Thailand and some Thai men may like to show off their foreign girlfriend. Still, as a foreign woman, you will make a better impression if you follow the traditional norms against displaying affection publicly.

Strange to many foreigners is the fact that, while public physical contact between men and women is looked down upon, physical contact between adults of the same sex is perfectly acceptable. It's not unusual to see two men walking along holding hands or women hugging each other. It doesn't necessarily mean they're gay— they are just being friendly.

NOTES

CHAPTER FIVE
Making Love

"Is sex dirty?" "Only if it's done right." —WOODY ALLEN,
Everything You Always Wanted to Know about Sex

◆ Give me a hug.　　　　　gɔ̀ɔt pǒm/chán nɔ̀i.
　　　　　　　　　　　　กอดผม/ฉันหน่อย

◆ May I hug you?　　　　　kɔ̌ɔ gɔ̀ɔt dâai mái?
　　　　　　　　　　　　ขอกอดได้มั้ย?

◆ May I kiss you?　　　　　kɔ̌ɔ jùup dâai mái?
　　　　　　　　　　　　ขอจูบได้มั้ย?

◆   You can kiss me.   jùup dâai.
                                        จูบได้

◆   Hold me tight.   gɔ̀ɔt nên-nên.
                                        กอดแน่นๆ

◆   Touch me here.   jàp dtrong níi.
                                        จับตรงนี้

◆   Touch me softly.   jàp bao-bao.
                                        จับเบาๆ

◆   Don't touch me.   yàa maa jàp pǒm/chán.
                                        อย่ามาจับผม/ฉัน

◆   You smell very good.   hɔ̌ɔm mâak.
                                        หอมมาก

◆   I like to feel you.   pǒm/chán chɔ̂ɔp jàp kun.
                                        ผม/ฉันชอบจับคุณ

◆   Your body is soft.   dtua kun nûm jang.
                                        ตัวคุณนุ่มจัง

◆   May I "sniff kiss" you?   kɔ̌ɔ hɔ̌ɔm dâai mái?
                                        ขอหอมได้มั้ย?

◆   Give me a "sniff kiss".   hɔ̌ɔm gêɛm.
                                        หอมแก้ม

Sniff Kissing

A "sniff kiss" is the traditional Thai romantic kiss. You plant your nose on your loved one's cheek (or other part of the body) and gently sniff in. Thai people consider this very sweet and romantic. It is also used by parents to show affection for their children. In general, men tend to "sniff kiss" their lovers more than women do. Lips on lips western style kissing is a relatively recent introduction, but is increasingly popular between lovers. Nevertheless, if you learn to "sniff kiss", your Thai lover will certainly appreciate it and be very pleased!

◆ Don't be shy.

mâi dtông aai.
ไม่ต้องอาย

◆ This is my first time.

kráng rêɛk kɔ̌ɔng pǒm/chán.
ครั้งแรกของผม/ฉัน

◆ I never slept with a Caucasian before.

mâi kəəi nɔɔn gàp fa-ràng.
ไม่เคยนอนกับฝรั่ง

◆ I never slept with a foreigner before.

mâi kəəi nɔɔn gàp chaao dtàang châat.
ไม่เคยนอนกับชาวต่างชาติ

◆ I want to sleep with you.

yàak nɔɔn gàp kun.
อยากนอนกับคุณ

◆ I don't want to sleep alone.

mâi yàak nɔɔn kon diao.
ไม่อยากนอนคนเดียว

◆ I don't want to do it now.   yang mâi yàak yûng
                                      dtɔɔn níi.
                                  ยังไม่อยากยุ่งตอนนี้

◆ Are you in the mood?   mii aa-rom mái?
                                  มีอารมณ์มั้ย?

◆ I'm horny (in the mood).   mii aa-rom.
                                  มีอารมณ์

◆ I'm not in the mood.   mâi mii aa-rom.
                                  ไม่มีอารมณ์

◆ You have a nice body.   kun hùn dii mâak.
                                  คุณหุ่นดีมาก

◆ Your skin is soft.   p̌iu kun nûm mâak.
                                  ผิวคุณนุ่มมาก

◆ Take your _____ off.   tɔ̀ɔt _____.
                                  ถอด

        bra   yók-song ยกทรง
        clothes   sɨ̂a-pâa เสื้อผ้า
        dress   chút ชุด
        pants   gaang-geeng กางเกง
        shoes   rɔɔng-táao รองเท้า
        skirt   gra-bproong กระโปรง
        underwear   gaang-geeng nai กางเกงใน

Body Parts

anus	dtùut ตูด
armpit	rák-rέε รักแร้
arm	kĕεn แขน
beard	krao เครา
belly	pung พุง
body	dtua ตัว
bottom	gôn ก้น
breast	nom นม
chest	òk อก
clitoris	bpùp-gra-săn ปุ่มกระสัน
dimple	lákyím ลักยิ้ม
ear	hŭu หู
eye	dtaa ตา
face	nâa หน้า
finger	níu นิ้วมือ
hair	pŏm ผม
head	hŭa หัว
heart	hŭa-jai หัวใจ
leg	kăa ขา
lips	rim fĭi bpàak ริมฝีปาก
mouth	bpàak ปาก
mustache	nùat หนวด
nail	lép เล็บ
navel	sa-dɯɯ สะดือ
neck	kɔɔ คอ
nipple	hŭa-nom หัวนม
nose	ja-mùuk จมูก
penis	ong-ka-châat องคชาติ

skin	pǐu ผิว
testicle	lûuk antá ลูกอัณฑะ
toes	níu-táao นิ้วเท้า
tongue	lín ลิ้น
tooth	fan ฟัน
throat	lamkɔɔ ลำคอ
vagina	chɔ̂ng-klɔ̂ɔt ช่องคลอด

Actions

arouse	grà-dtûn กระตุ้น
bite	gàt กัด
blow	bpào เป่า
caress	láo-loom เล้าโลม
caress tenderly	klʉng คลึง
cry	rɔ́ɔng-hâai ร้องไห้
dance	dtên เต้น
dream	fǎn ฝัน
to become excited	dtʉ̀ʉn-dtên ตื่นเต้น
to fantasize	jinta-naa-gaan จินตนาการ
feel hurt	jèp เจ็บ
feel the thrill	sǐao เสียว
feel stinging pain	sɛ̀ɛp แสบ
force	bangkáp บังคับ
gasp	hɔ̀ɔp หอบ
groan	kruan-kraang ครวญคราง
hug	gɔ̀ɔt กอด
hurt (someone)	tam hâi jèp ทำให้เจ็บ
be in the mood	mii aa-rom มีอารมณ์
insert	sɔ̀ɔt สอด

kiss	jùup จูบ
lick	lia เลีย
lose one's virginity	sĭa-dtua เสียตัว
massage	nûat นวด
masturbate	chûai dtua-eeng ช่วยตัวเอง
moan	kraang คราง
pee	chĭi, yĭao ฉี่, เยี่ยว
penetrate	sĭap เสียบ
perform oral sex	tam ɔɔ-rân ทำออรัล
rape	kòm-kŭɯn ข่มขืน
resist	kàt-kŭɯn ขัดขืน
rest	pákpɔ̀n พักผ่อน
rouse	bplùk aa-rom ปลุกอารมณ์
be satisfied	samrèt kwaamkrai สำเร็จความใคร่
scream	rɔ́ɔng-gríit ร้องกรี๊ด
shake	sàn สั่น
shave	goon โกน
sleep	nɔɔn นอน
smell (n.)	glìn กลิ่น
smell (v.)	dom ดม
squeeze	bĭip บีบ
suck	dùut ดูด
surrender	yinyɔɔm ยินยอม
tease	yûa ยั่ว
tickle/ticklish	ják-ga-jĭi จั๊กจี้
torture	tɔɔ-ra-maan ทรมาณ
touch	jàp จับ
urinate	pàtsawá ปัสสาวะ

Other Useful Vocabulary

abortion	tam-téng ทำแท้ง
afraid	glua กลัว
AIDS	rôok èet โรคเอดส์
anal sex	rûap pêet taang ta-waan ร่วมเพศทางทวาร
bathtub	àang-náam อ่างน้ำ
bar girl	pûu-yǐng baa ผู้หญิงบาร์
bed	dtiang เตียง
bisexual	chɔ̂ɔp tâng sɔ̌ɔng pêet ชอบทั้งสองเพศ
blanket	pâa-hòm ผ้าห่ม
catch a disease	dtìt-rôok ติดโรค
concubine	naang-bam-rəə นางบำเรอ
condom	tǔng-yaang ถุงยาง kɔndôm คอนด้อม
contraceptive	yaa-kum ยาคุม
contract (vagina, etc.)	ka-mǐp ขมิบ
desire (for sex)	kwaam krâi ความใคร่
distasteful	nâa-glìat น่าเกลียด
dildo	kɔ̌ɔng-tiam ของเทียม
dirty	sòk-ga-bpròk สกปรก
disease	rôok โรค
fat	ûan อ้วน
gay	gee เกย์
hard	kěng แข็ง
homosexual	chɔ̂ɔp pêet diao gan ชอบเพศเดียวกัน
hole	ruu รู
lesbian	lesbian เลสเบียน

lubricant	náam lɔ̀-lʉ̂ʉn น้ำหล่อลื่น
lust	dtanhǎa ตัณหา
lustful	dtanhǎa jàt ตัณหาจัด
	bâa-gaam บ้ากาม
masseuse, massuer	mɔ̌ɔ-nûat หมอนวด
menstruation	bpra-jam-dʉan ประจำเดือน
mistress	mia-nɔ́ɔi เมียน้อย
mood	aa-rom อารมณ์
naked	lɔ̂njɔ̂n ล่อนจ้อน
oral sex	châi bpàak ใช้ปาก
orgasm	jùt sùt yɔ̂ɔt จุดสุดยอด
orgy	sék-mùu เซ็กซ์หมู่
pillow	mɔ̌ɔn หมอน
pillow case	bplɔ̀ɔk mɔ̌ɔn ปลอกหมอน
pregnant	mii-tɔ́ɔng มีท้อง
prostitute	soo-pee-nii โสเภณี
semen	náam a-su-jì น้ำอสุจิ
sexual disease	rôok taang pêet โรคทางเพศ
sex toys	kɔ̌ɔng lên taang pêet
	ของเล่นทางเพศ
sexual desire	gaammaa-rom กามารมณ์
sexual pervert	gaamwit-dtà-tǎan กามวิตถาร
sexy	séksǐi เซ็กซี่
sexy movie	nǎng-bpóo หนังโป๊
shameful	bàtsǐi บัดสี
sheet (bed)	pâa-bpuu fii-nɔɔn ผ้าปูที่นอน
soak (ed)	bpìak chôok เปียกโชค
soap	sa-bùu สบู่
soft	nûm, ɔ̀ɔn นุ่ม, อ่อน
sperm	a-su-jì อสุจิ

strong	kĕng-rɛɛng แข็งแรง
tender	ɔ̀ɔn-yoon อ่อนโยน
thin	pɔ̌ɔm ผอม
towel	pâa-chét-dtua ผ้าเช็ดตัว
transvestite	ga-təəi กะเทย
venereal disease	gaamma-rôok กามโรค
virgin	bɔɔ-ri-sùt บริสุทธิ์
wet	bpĭak เปียก

See slang, colloquialisms and profanity in Chapter Nine — Night Life.

Virginity

To an unescorted foreign male visiting Thailand it may seem at times that whenever he steps out of his hotel he is pursued by an endless stream of pimps and procurers selling him various sexual services. To speak of the importance of virginity to Thai women in this environment may appear a bit of an oxymoron. Nevertheless, it is true that traditional Thai women are actually very conservative about sex. Women were supposed to keep their virginity until the day they married. Although the country has changed a lot with modernization and contact with western civilization and while many Thai women are quite open to sex, there are still quite a few who stay virgins as long as they are single— on into their 20's, 30's, 40's and older. They believe that they should save themselves for their one and only true love. Most wealthy and elite families (and those that emulate them) are very protective of their daughters, who are expected to live at home under the watchful eyes of family members until they marry. Sex is a taboo subject. Sometimes these women are still afraid to express their feelings in bed even after they are married. Others may be glad for the opportunity to escape the restrictive confines of Thai high society.

Young Thai men, meanwhile, are generally given freer rein. The large numbers of brothels, massage par girlie bars offer ample opportunity for sexual experimentat an early age.

◆ I'm still a virgin.

pŏm/chán yang bɔɔ-ri-sùt.
ผม/ฉันยังบริสุทธิ์

◆ I masturbate sometimes.

baang-tii pŏm/chán chûai dtua-eeng.
บางทีผม/ฉันช่วยตัวเอง

◆ You have beautiful breasts.

nom sŭai.
นมสวย

◆ Would you like to take a bath (shower)?

àap-náam mái?
อาบน้ำมั้ย

Cleanliness

Personal cleanliness is very important to Thai people. Since Thailand is a hot, humid country people tend to get sweaty and dirty very quickly. Taking two or three showers a day is quite common and most Thai like to bathe before making love. Even though you may not feel that you are dirty, it's usually best to accept an invitation to take a shower or a bath before any sexual interlude. Your Thai lover will feel much better about you and more confident making love if (s)he knows that both of you are clean.

◆ Use your mouth on me.

chái bpàak hâi nɔ̀i.
ใช้ปากให้หน่อย

◆ I like oral sex.

chɔ̂ɔp ɔɔ-rân sék.
ชอบออรัลเซ็กซ์

◆ I don't like oral sex.

mâi chɔ̂ɔp ɔɔ-rân sék.
ไม่ชอบออรัลเซ็กซ์

◆ You've got a big one.

kɔ̌ɔng kun yài jang.
ของคุณใหญ่จัง

◆ It is so hard.

man kěng dii jang.
มันแข็งดีจัง

◆ Use a condom.

chái tǔng-yaang.
ใช้ถุงยาง

◆ Don't forget to put a condom on.

yàa lɯɯm sài tǔng-yaang.
อย่าลืมใส่ถุงยาง

◆ I don't want to get a disease.

mâi yàak dtìt rôok.
ไม่อยากติดโรค

◆ I don't want to get pregnant.

mâi yàak mii tɔ́ɔng.
ไม่อยากมีท้อง

◆ I'm afraid of getting pregnant.

glua mii tɔ́ɔng.
กลัวมีท้อง

◆ Do you have any diseases?

kun mii rôok mái?
คุณมีโรคมั้ย

◆   Do you use birth control?   kun chái yaa kum mái?
                                       คุณกินยาคุมมั้ย?

◆   Are you taking pills?   kun gin yaa kum yùu mái?
                                       คุณกินยาคุมอยู่มั้ย?

◆   Is it safe for you today?   wanníi bplɔ̀ɔt-pai mái?
                                       วันนี้ปลอดภัยมั้ย?

◆   I don't like condoms.   pǒm/chán mâi chɔ̂ɔp
                                           tǔng-yaang.
                                       ผม/ฉันไม่ชอบถุงยาง

◆   We should use a condom.   rao kuan chái tǔng-yaang.
                                       เราควรใช้ถุงยาง

◆   We must use a condom.   rao dtɔ̂ng chái tǔng-yaang.
                                       เราต้องใช้ถุงยาง

◆   I'm afraid of AIDS.   glua dtìt èet.
                                       กลัวติดเอดส์

◆   Let's watch an adult video.   duu nǎng-bpóo gan tə̀.
                                       ดูหนังโป๊กันเถอะ

◆   I like to watch adult videos.   chɔ̂ɔp duu nǎng-bpóo.
                                       ชอบดูหนังโป๊

◆   Gently!   bao-bao.
                                       เบาๆ

◆ Not so hard.

yàa tam runrɛɛng.

อย่าทำรุนแรง

◆ I like it gentle.

chɔ̂ɔp bao-bao.

ชอบเบาๆ

◆ I like it hard.

chɔ̂ɔp rɛɛng-rɛɛng.

ชอบแรงๆ

◆ Does it hurt?

jèp mái?

เจ็บมั้ย?

● Yes, it hurts.

jèp.

เจ็บ

● No, it doesn't hurt.

mâi jèp.

ไม่เจ็บ

◆ That feels good.

rúu-sʉ̀k dii.

รู้สึกดี

◆ What position do you like?

kun chɔ̂ɔp tâa nǎi?

คุณชอบท่าไหน?

◆ I like this style.

chɔ̂ɔp tâa níi.

ชอบท่านี้

◆ I like the rear-entry position. ("doggy style")

chɔ̂ɔp tâa lǎng.

ชอบท่าหลัง

◆ 69 is my favorite position.

chɔ̂ɔp tâa hòk-sǐp-gâao tii-sùt.

ชอบท่าหกสิบเก้าที่สุด

◆ I like you being on top.   chɔ̂ɔp hâi kun
                                   bon.
                               ชอบให้คุณอยู่ข้างบน

◆ What turns you on?   a-rai tamhâi kun   ...ɔm?
                               อะไรทำให้คุณมีอารมณ์?

◆ Did you come?   kun sèt mái?
                               คุณเสร็จมั้ย?

◆ I'm coming.   jà sèt lɛ́ɛo.
                               จะเสร็จแล้ว

◆ I came.   sèt lɛ́ɛo.
                               เสร็จแล้ว

◆ I came twice.   sèt sɔ̌ɔng kráng.
                               เสร็จสองครั้ง

◆ I came twice last night.   mûa-kʉʉn-níi sèt sɔ̌ɔng
                                   kráng.
                               เมื่อคืนนี้เสร็จสองครั้ง

To Have an Orgasm

The word sèt (เสร็จ) in Thai means both "to finish" and "to come" or have an orgasm. Sometimes Thai people translate it into English directly. They may ask you, "Are you finished?" instead of "Did you come?". We have an American friend who was very offended that his Thai girlfriend always asked him if he was finished

ⱼ ₍ever they made love. He thought that she wanted him to fin-
ₛh the love-making as fast as possible and that she was not enjoy-
ing it with him. He laughed and felt much better after we explained
the meaning of sèt (เสร็จ) to him.

◆ You were very good.

kun tam gèng mâak.
คุณทำเก่งมาก

◆ I feel good.

rúu-sùk sa-baai.
รู้สึกสบาย

◆ Shall we do it again?

ao-ìik mái?
เอาอีกมั้ย?

◆ Just a minute.

rɔɔ dǐao.
รอเดี๋ยว

◆ Let me rest for a while.

kɔ̌ɔ pák bpép nùng.
ขอพักแป๊บนึง

◆ I'm ready.

prɔ́ɔm lɛ́ɛo.
พร้อมแล้ว

◆ I need to get hard.

dtɔ̂ng hâi kèng gɔ̀ɔn.
ต้องให้แข็งก่อน

◆ That was fun.

sa-nùk mâak.
สนุกมาก

Please practice safe sex!

CHAPTER SIX
Love Letters

"At the touch of love, everyone becomes a poet." —PLATO, *Symposium*

With modern telecommunications it's often possible to have frequent telephone conversations with your Thai lover from practically anywhere in the world. Many Thais, however, don't have easy access to a private phone. Also, the language barrier is especially difficult to overcome in a phone conversation. With a letter you are able to express your thoughts and feelings in a form that can be understood more clearly by the reader. Surely no telephone conversation can match the feeling you get when reading a love letter over and over again! Some people in Thailand have access to a fax machine or e-mail. In that case, you shouldn't have to wait weeks or even days to exchange letters. If your Thai lover has translation and fax expenses, you may want to offer to pay for them. Following are some examples of love letters, including greetings, closes, common words used in writing letters and some sample sentences that you can try copying in the Thai alphabet. The Thai alphabet is shown in large print for your convenience in the appendix of this book. (For a complete introduction to the Thai writing system see "Thai for Beginners").

Sample Love Letters

Dear Supa,

How are you doing? I am doing well except I miss you very much back here in America. I had a wonderful time with you and your friends in Bangkok. Thank you very much for taking me around.

I want to call you once a week. Please let me know a good time for me to call. I want to hear your voice and know how you are doing.

I hope you understand this letter. If not, you can have it translated. It would be nice if you could take an English class so that we could communicate better.

Please take care of yourself. I look forward to hearing from you soon.

With love,

Peter

Translation

สุภา ที่รัก

    เป็นยังไงบ้าง ผมสบายดีแต่ว่าคิดถึงคุณมากหลังจากที่
กลับมาอเมริกาแล้ว ผมสนุกมากที่ได้ใช้เวลาที่กรุงเทพกับคุณ
และเพื่อนของคุณ ขอบคุณมากที่พาผมไปเที่ยวที่ต่างๆ

    ผมอยากโทรมาหาคุณอาทิตย์ละครั้ง ช่วยบอกผมด้วยว่า
เวลาไหนที่จะคุณสะดวก ผมต้องการได้ยินเสียงคุณและถามทุก
สุขของคุณ

    ผมหวังว่าคุณคงเข้าใจจดหมายฉบับนี้ ถ้าคุณไม่เข้าใจ
ก็ให้หาคนช่วยแปล ผมคิดว่าจะดีมากถ้าคุณเข้าเรียนภาษา
อังกฤษเพื่อที่เราจะสามารถสื่อสารกันได้ดีขึ้น

    กรุณารักษาสุขภาพ ผมหวังว่าจะได้รับคำตอบจากคุณ
ในเร็วๆ นี้

ด้วยรัก

ปีเตอร์

Dearest Peter,

I was so happy to receive your letter. I was wondering when you would contact me. I am doing well. It rained yesterday, but it's still very hot in Bangkok today.

Peter, I miss you very much also. I want to see you again soon. When will you come to Thailand again?

You can call me after six o'clock in the evening. I get home about five thirty. I don't know what time it is in America then. If it's not a good time, you can call me in the morning. I get up at five and leave home at seven o'clock.

I had a friend translate your letter and write this letter for me. I want to learn English in a language school here, but the lessons are expensive. I'm learning from some books at this time.

I hope you are doing fine. Take care of your health and don't work too hard.

Love and miss you,

Supa

Translation

ปีเตอร์ สุดที่รัก

ฉันดีใจมากที่ได้รับจดหมายจากคุณ ฉันรออยู่ว่าคุณจะ
ติดต่อมาอีกเมื่อไหร่ ฉันสบายดี เมื่อวานนี้ฝนตกแต่วันนี้อากาศ
ที่กรุงเทพร้อนมาก

ปีเตอร์ ฉันก็คิดถึงคุณมากเช่นเดียวกัน ฉันอยากจะพบ
คุณอีกเร็วๆ คุณจะมาเมืองไทยอีกเมื่อไหร่

คุณโทรมาหาฉันได้หลังหกโมงเย็น ฉันกลับบ้าน
ประมาณห้าโมงครึ่ง ฉันไม่รู้ว่าเวลาที่อเมริกากี่โมง ถ้าไม่สะดวก
คุณโทรมาตอนเช้าก็ได้ ฉันตื่นนอนตอนตีห้าและออกจากบ้าน
ตอนเจ็ดโมงเช้า

ฉันให้เพื่อนแปลจดหมายของคุณและเขียนจดหมายฉบับ
นี้ให้ ฉันต้องการเรียนภาษาอังกฤษที่โรงเรียนสอนภาษา แต่ค่า
เรียนแพงมาก ตอนนี้ฉันกำลังเรียนจากหนังสือ

ฉันหวังว่าคุณคงสบายดีนะ ขอให้รักษาสุขภาพและก็
อย่าทำงานหนักเกินไป

รักและคิดถึง

สุภา

Letter Greetings

Dear.....   .....ที่รัก
                                    (tîi-rák)

Dearest.....   .....สุดที่รัก
                                    (sùt tîi-rák)

My dear.....   .....ที่รักของ<u>ผม</u>/ฉัน
                                    (tîi-rák kɔ̌ɔng
                                        <u>pǒm</u>/chán)

Hello.....   สวัสดี.....
                                    (sa-wàt-dii)

To.....   ถึง.....
                                    (tǔng)

Closing

Love   รัก
                                    (rák)

Love always   รักเสมอ
                                    (rák sa-mɔ̌ə)

Love you   รักคุณ
                                    (rák kun)

Love and miss you   รักและคิดถึง
                                    (rák lɛ́ kíttǔng)

With love	ด้วยรัก
	(dûai rák)
Thinking about you	คิดถึงเสมอ
always	(kíttǔng sa-mǒə)
Your friend	เพื่อนของคุณ
	(pûan kɔ̌ɔng kun)

Word List

address	tîi-yùu ที่อยู่
apologize	kɔ̌ɔ-tôot ขอโทษ
bank	ta-naa-kaan ธนาคาร
busy	yûng ยุ่ง
buy	súu ซื้อ
call (v.)	too โทร
cheap	tùuk ถูก
cold	nǎao หนาว
come	maa มา
difficult	yâak ยาก
disappointed	pìtwǎng ผิดหวัง
easy	ngâai ง่าย
English	paa-šaa ang-grìt ภาษาอังกฤษ
envelope	sɔɔng jòtmǎai ซองจดหมาย
e-mail	ii-meeo อีเมล์
expensive	pɛɛng แพง
express mail	jòtmǎai-dùan จดหมายด่วน
fax	fɛ̀ɛk แฟ็กซ์
gift	kɔ̌ɔng-kwǎn ของขวัญ

glad	dii-jai ดีใจ
go	bpai ไป
family	krɔ̂ɔpkrua ครอบครัว
forget	luum ลืม
happy	mii-kwaamsùk มีความสุข
healthy	sùkka-pâap-dii สุขภาพดี
holiday	wan-yùt วันหยุด
home, house	bâan บ้าน
honey (loved one)	tîi-rák ที่รัก
hot	rɔ́ɔn ร้อน
hotel	roong-rɛɛm โรงแรม
know	rúu รู้
have	mii มี
internet	in-dtəə-nèt อินเตอร์เน็ท
language	paa-sǎa ภาษา
letter	jòt-mǎai จดหมาย
listen	fang ฟัง
long distance call	too-taang glai โทรทางไกล
love	rák รัก
miss	kíttǔng คิดถึง
misunderstand	kâo-jai-pìt เข้าใจผิด
money	ngən เงิน
much, many, very	mâak มาก
opportunity	oo-gàat โอกาส
pay	jàai จ่าย
picture	rûup รูป
plan	waang-pěɛn วางแผน
problem	bpan-hǎa ปัญหา
proud	puum-jai ภูมิใจ
read	àan อ่าน
remember	jam-dâai จำได้
relationship	kwaamsǎm-pan ความสัมพันธ์

return	glàp กลับ
responsible	ráp-pìt-chɔ̂ɔp รับผิดชอบ
send	sòng ส่ง
sign (name)	sen-chน̂น เซ็นชื่อ
signature	laai-sen ลายเซ็น
sorry	sǐa-jai เสียใจ
speak	pûut พูด
spell	sa-gòt สะกด
spend money	chái-ngən ใช้เงิน
spend time	chái-wee-laa ใช้เวลา
stamp	sa-dtɛm แสตมป์
study	rian เรียน
take care of	duu-lɛɛ ดูแล
teach	sɔ̌ɔn สอน
telephone	too-ra-sàp โทรศัพท์
tell	bɔ̀ɔk บอก
Thai	tai ไทย
Thai language	paa-saa-tai ภาษาไทย
think about	kíttน̌ng คิดถึง
this letter	jòtmǎai cha-bàp níi
	จดหมายฉบับนี้
together	dûai-gan ด้วยกัน
transfer money	oon-ngən โอนเงิน
translate	bplɛɛ แปล
translator	pûu-bplɛɛ ผู้แปล
travel	dəəntaang เดินทาง
trip	gaan dəəntaang การเดินทาง
vacation	yùt pák-rɔ́ɔn หยุดพักร้อน
weather	aa-gàat อากาศ
work	tam-ngaan ทำงาน
worry	gang-won กังวล
write	kǐan เขียน

Sample Sentences for Love Letters

       Here are some sentences you can try copying in the Thai alphabet. Even if you can't write Thai very well, the effort you've made will surely create a good impression. Male writers should use pŏm (ผม) and females chán (ฉัน) for the first person "I" pronoun which is indicated by the underline.

Note: Thai does not use a period to end sentences. Instead, phrases and sentences are seperated by a space (there is no space between words, which all run together). Question marks and commas are sometimes used, but not commonly.

◆ I miss you very much.
    <u>pŏm</u>/<u>chán</u> kít-tǔng kun mâak.

    <u>ผม</u>/<u>ฉัน</u>คิดถึงคุณมาก

◆ How have you been doing?
    bpen yang-ngai bâang?

    เป็นยังไงบ้าง

◆ I'm doing well.
    <u>pŏm</u>/<u>chán</u> sa-baai-dii.

    <u>ผม</u>/<u>ฉัน</u>สบายดี

◆ How is the weather over there?
    aa-gàat tîi-nân bpen yang-ngai bâang?

    อากาศที่นั่นเป็นยังไงบ้าง

◆ It's very cold here.
dtɔɔnníi aa-gàat tîi-nîi nǎao mâak.
ตอนนี้อากาศที่นี่หนาวมาก

◆ How is your family?
krɔ̂ɔpkrua kun bpen yang-ngai bâang.
ครอบครัวคุณเป็นยังไงบ้าง

◆ Happy Birthday!
sùksǎn wan gə̀ət!
สุขสันต์วันเกิด

◆ Happy Valentine's Day!
sùksǎn wan waa-leen-tain!
สุขสันต์วันวาเลนไทน์

◆ Merry Christmas and Happy New Year!
sùksǎn wan krítsa-mât lé bpii-mài!
สุขสันต์วันคริสต์มาสและปีใหม่

◆ I want you to send me some pictures.
pǒm/chán yàak hâi kun sòng rûup maa hâi duu.
ผม/ฉันอยากให้คุณส่งรูปมาให้ดู

◆   The pictures you sent me are very nice.
    rûup fii kun sòng maa sŭai mâak.

รูปที่คุณส่งมาสวยมาก

◆   I'm sorry for taking so long to write back.
    kɔ̌ɔ-tôot fii dtɔ̀ɔp jòtmăai kɔ̌ɔng kun cháa.

ขอโทษที่ตอบจดหมายของคุณช้า

◆   I want to go to Thailand again soon.
    yàak bpai mɯang tai ʔìik reo-reo.

อยากไปเมืองไทยอีกเร็วๆ

◆   I want to be with you again as soon as possible.
    pŏm/chán yàak póp gàp kun ʔìik hâi reo fii-sùt.

ผม/ฉันอยากพบกับคุณอีกให้เร็วที่สุด

◆   I miss you very much after coming back from Thailand.
    glàp jàak mɯang tai lɛ́ɛo kíttŭng kun mâak.

กลับจากเมืองไทยแล้วคิดถึงคุณมาก

◆   I'm very lonely without you here.
    pŏm/chán ngăo mâak mɯ̂a mâi mii kun yùu fii-nîi.

ผม/ฉันเหงามากเมื่อไม่มีคุณอยู่ที่นี่

◆ I want you to come to America.

pǒm/chán yàak hâi kun maa-hǎa fii a-mee-ri-kaa.

ผม/ฉันอยากให้คุณมาหาที่อเมริกา

◆ I'm working very hard now.

dtɔɔn-níi pǒm/chán tam-ngaan nàk mâak.

ตอนนี้ผม/ฉันทำงานหนักมาก

◆ I don't want you to work hard.

pǒm/chán mâi yàak hâi kun tam-ngaan nàk.

ผม/ฉันไม่อยากให้คุณทำงานหนัก

◆ I don't have any vacation yet.

dtɔɔn-níi yang mâi mii wan-yùt.

ตอนนี้ยังไม่มีวันหยุด

◆ I will send you some money to study English.

pǒm/chán jà sòng ngən hâi kun rian paa-šaa ang-grìt.

ผม/ฉันจะส่งเงินไปให้คุณเรียนภาษาอังกฤษ

◆ I want to study the Thai language.

pǒm/chán yàak jà rian paa-sǎa tai.

ผม/ฉันอยากจะเรียนภาษาไทย

◆ I'm studying Thai at a Thai temple.

<u>pŏm/chán</u> gamlang rian paa-săa tai ɡi wát tai.

<u>ผม/ฉัน</u>กำลังเรียนภาษาไทยที่วัดไทย

◆ Today I had Thai food at a restaurant.

wanníi bpai taan aa-hăan tai ɡi ráan aa-hăan.

วันนี้ไปทานอาหารไทยที่ร้านอาหาร

◆ I tell everybody about you.

<u>pŏm/chán</u> lâo rûang kɔ̌ɔng kun hâi túk kon fang.

<u>ผม/ฉัน</u>เล่าเรื่องของคุณให้ทุกคนฟัง

◆ I want to write you often, but I don't have much time.

yàak kĭan tŭng kun bɔ̀i-bɔ̀i, dtɛ̀ɛ mâi kɔ̂i mii wee-laa.

อยากเขียนถึงคุณบ่อยๆ แต่ไม่ค่อยมีเวลา

◆ I will go to Thailand again in two months.

<u>pŏm/chán</u> jà bpai mʉang tai ˇiik sɔ̌ɔng dʉan.

<u>ผม/ฉัน</u>จะไปเมืองไทยอีกสองเดือน

◆ I want you to pick me up at the airport.

<u>pŏm/chán</u> yàak hâi kun maa ráp ɡi sa-năambin.

<u>ผม/ฉัน</u>อยากให้คุณมารับที่สนามบิน

◆ I will call you when I arrive in Thailand.
jà too tŭng kun mûa tŭng mɯang tai lɛ́ɛo.

จะโทรถึงคุณเมื่อถึงเมืองไทยแล้ว

◆ I will go to Thailand again on (day) ____ (month)____.
pŏm/chán jà bpai mɯang tai ʼìik wan tîi ____ dɯan ____.

ผม/ฉันจะไปเมืองไทยอีกวันที่ ___ เดือน ___

◆ The flight number is ____
tîao-bin tîi ____.

เที่ยวบินที่ ___

◆ Please reply as soon as possible.
dâai-ráp lɛ́ɛo dtɔ̀ɔp dùan dûai.

ได้รับแล้วตอบด่วนด้วย

◆ I will wait for your reply.
pŏm/chán jà rɔɔ kam-dtɔ̀ɔp jàak kun.

ผม/ฉันจะรอคำตอบจากคุณ

◆ I hope everyone is doing well.
wăng wâa túk kon kong sa-baai-dii.

หวังว่าทุกคนคงสบายดี

◆   Please give my best regards to _____.
     fàak kwaam kíttǔng tǔng _____ dûai.

ฝากความคิดถึงถึง _____ ด้วย

◆   Take care of your health.
     kɔ̌ɔ hâi ráksǎa sùkka-pâap.

ขอให้รักษาสุขภาพ

◆   I wish you good luck.
     kɔ̌ɔ hâi kun chôkdii.

ขอให้คุณโชคดี

CHAPTER SEVEN
Getting Married

"It doesn't much signify whom one marries, for one is sure to find next morning that it was someone else." —SAMUEL RODGERS, *Table Talk*

◆ I want to marry you.

pŏm/chán yàak
dtèng-ngaan gàp kun.
ผม/ฉันอยากแต่งงานกับคุณ

◆ Marry me.

dtèng-ngaan gàp pŏm/chán
tè-ná.
แต่งงานกับผม/ฉันเถอะนะ

◆ Do you want to marry me?   yàak dtèng-ngaan gàp
                                         pŏm/chán mái?
                                     คุณอยากแต่งงานกับผม/ฉันมั้ย?

  ● Very much.   yàak mâak ləəi.
                                     อยากมากเลย

  ● I'd rather wait.   rɔɔ-duu gɔ̀ɔn.
                                     รอดูก่อน

  ● Let me think about it.   kŏɔ kít duu gɔ̀ɔn.
                                     ขอคิดดูก่อน

  ● Give me some more time.   kŏɔ wee-laa nɔ̀i.
                                     ขอเวลาหน่อย

  ● I don't want to get   pŏm/chán yang mâi yàak
    married yet.   dtèng-ngaan.
                                     ผม/ฉันยังไม่อยากแต่งงาน

◆ Are you sure you want to   kun nɛ̂ɛ-jai rɯ́ wâa kun
  marry me?   yàak dtèng-ngaan gàp
                                         pŏm/chán?
                                     คุณแน่ใจรึว่าอยากแต่งงานกับผม/ฉัน?

◆ I want to have a family soon.   yàak mii krɔ̂ɔp-krua
                                         reo-reo.
                                     อยากมีครอบครัวเร็วๆ

◆ I want to get married before   yàak dtèng-ngaan gɔ̀ɔn ɗii
  I'm too old.   jà gɛ̀ɛ gəən bpai.
                                     อยากแต่งงานก่อนที่จะแก่เกินไป

◆ It's time to get married.   tʉ̌ng wee-laa ɗii jà
                                         dtèng-ngaan lɛ́ɛo.
                                     ถึงเวลาที่จะแต่งงานแล้ว

◆ I was married before.   pǒm/chán kəəi dtɛ̀ng-ngaan
                       maa gɔ̀ɔn.
                       ผม/ฉันเคยแต่งงานมาก่อน

◆ I'm divorced.   pǒm/chán yàa lɛ́ɛo.
                       ผม/ฉันหย่าแล้ว

◆ I don't want to live alone anymore.   mâi yàak yùu kon diao
                       ʼiik dtɔ̀ɔ-bpai.
                       ไม่อยากอยู่คนเดียวอีกต่อไป

◆ I don't want to wait anymore.   mâi yàak rɔɔ ʼiik dtɔ̀ɔ-bpai.
                       ไม่อยากรออีกต่อไป

◆ Why aren't you married?   tammai kun mâi
                       dtɛ̀ng-ngaan?
                       ทำไมคุณไม่แต่งงาน?

● I haven't met anyone like you before.   yang mâi jəə kon yàng kun.
                       ยังไม่เจอคนอย่างคุณ

● I haven't found anyone I really like yet.   yang mâi jəə kon ɦi chɔ̂ɔp
                       jing-jing.
                       ยังไม่เจอคนที่ชอบจริงๆ

◆ You are the one I've been waiting for.   kun bpen kon ɦi pǒm/chán
                       rɔɔ maa-naan.
                       คุณเป็นคนที่ผม/ฉันรอมานาน

◆ You are the one I want to spend the rest of my life with.   kun bpen kon ɦi pǒm/chán
                       yàak yùu dûai dta-lɔ̀ɔt
                       chii-wít.
                       คุณเป็นคนที่ผม/ฉันอยากอยู่ด้วย
                       ตลอดชีวิต

◆   I promise to make you happy.   pŏm/chán săn-yaa wâa
                                     jà tam hâi kun mii
                                     kwaam sùk.
                                     ผม/ฉันสัญญาว่าจะทำให้คุณมี
                                     ความสุข

Meeting the Family

It may seem that a section on meeting the family should be in the chapter on courting. We decided to put it in "Getting Married" because it is considered a fairly serious step in Thailand. When a Thai brings you home and introduces you as a boyfriend or girlfriend to his/her parents, the family will probably start evaluating your potential as a marriage partner. What kind of family do you come from? Are you good hearted and responsible or a drunkard, gambler and wastrel? What's your education? Do you have a good job or business? What is your financial situation? Are you sincere or just in Thailand for a lark and then off to some far away land never to be heard from again? Since you are a foreigner, all these factors are harder for them to determine. You are out of the loop— the family's information grapevine probably doesn't extend abroad. The easy solution would be to reject you outright. Hopefully that won't happen and they will suspend judgement until they know more about you.

Naturally, you want to make the best impression you can. Your Thai partner will help you with this. Also, many of the better guide books have sections on Thai culture that would be worth reviewing. Here are a few tips:

❐   Be clean, well dressed and polite. If you are a man, short hair and being clean shaven are a plus. Smile!

❐   Speak softly and maintain a calm demeaner.

❏   Treat your Thai partner's parents with great respect. Even if they are poor, uneducated and have menial jobs, their position as parents of the person you are with gives them a special status.

❏   Follow the Thai cultural norms of not displaying physical affection in public. If there is any physical affection in front of others, let it be initiated by your Thai partner and not by you. If you are staying overnight in the area, let your Thai partner suggest the sleeping arrangements. Even if you have been sleeping together up until now, this will probably not be appropriate around the family. Don't feel slighted if you end up in a nearby hotel while your partner stays with the family.

❏   Always remove your shoes before entering a home or a Buddhist temple. Often this has nothing to do with the relative cleanliness of your shoes and the floor in question. Removing one's shoes is such a strong cultural imperative that to not do so would be considered insulting and boorish.

❏   Avoid pointing the bottoms of your feet at people. Thais often sit on the floor. Sitting cross-legged or with your feet tucked behind you are best. When sitting in a chair, keep your feet on the floor.

❏   Don't touch the heads of others. The head, as the highest part of the body, is considered sacred.

❏   Don't point at people with your finger. Pointing at people is considered rude.

❏   Thailand is overwhelmingly Buddhist. When meeting a monk, wai and show respect. If you are a woman, never touch a monk or his robes. While visiting a temple, do not sit pointing the bottoms of your feet towards the Buddha image or a monk. In this case you shouldn't sit cross-legged either. In front of a Buddha image or a monk sit with your feet tucked behind you.

❏ Avoid stepping on the threshold of a home or temple. Many Thais believe that the spirit of a building lives in the threshold of the entrance.

❏ Show appreciation for Thailand and things Thai. Be respectful of the Thai royal family and of Buddhism. Liking Thai food and trying to speak some Thai are bound to be points in your favor.

Finally, don't be so worried about doing everything right that you become culturally constipated. Relax and enjoy yourself. If you have a good heart and are sincere, almost all else will be forgiven. Thai people are very tolerant of foreigners and don't expect you to understand all their customs.

◆ I want you to meet my parents.   yàak paa kun bpai hăa
                                                               pɔ̂ɔ-mêɛ.
                                       อยากพาคุณไปหาพ่อแม่

◆ What will your parents think   pɔ̂ɔ-mêɛ kun jà kít
      about me?   yang-ngai gàp pŏm/chán?
                                       พ่อแม่คุณจะคิดยังไงกับผม/ฉัน?

◆ What will your family think   pɔ̂ɔ-mêɛ kun jà kít
      of you marrying a foreigner?   yang-ngai tîi kun
                                                   dtɛ̀ng-ngann gàp chaao-
                                                   dtàang-châat?
                                       พ่อแม่คุณจะคิดยังไงที่คุณแต่งงาน
                                       กับชาวต่างชาติ

◆ I think my parents will like you.

kít wâa pɔ̂ɔ-mɛ̂ɛ kɔ̌ɔng
    pǒm/chán jà chɔ̂ɔp kun.
คิดว่าพ่อ-แม่ของผม/ฉันจะชอบคุณ

◆ I don't want to leave Thailand.

mâi yàak jàak muang tai.
ไม่อยากจากเมืองไทย

◆ I want to live in Thailand after getting married.

yàak yùu muang tai lǎng
    dtɛ̀ng-ngaan.
อยากอยู่เมืองไทยหลังแต่งงาน

◆ I want to live abroad.

yàak yùu muang nɔ̂ɔk.
อยากอยู่เมืองนอก

◆ I don't want to live abroad.

mâi yàak yùu muang nɔ̂ɔk.
ไม่อยากอยู่เมืองนอก

◆ I have to ask my parents first.

dtɔ̂ng tǎam pɔ̂ɔ-mɛ̂ɛ
    duu gɔ̀ɔn.
ต้องถามพ่อ-แม่ดูก่อน

◆ You can make your own decision.

kun dtàt-sǐnjai eeng dâai.
คุณตัดสินใจเองได้

◆ You have to talk with my parents first.

kun dtɔ̂ng kui gàp pɔ̂ɔ-mɛ̂ɛ
    pǒm/chán gɔ̀ɔn.
คุณต้องคุยกับพ่อ-แม่ผม/ฉันก่อน

◆ I don't want to leave my parents.

mâi yàak tíng pɔ̂ɔ-mɛ̂ɛ.
ไม่อยากทิ้งพ่อ-แม่

◆ I have to support my family.   pǒm/chán dtôong chûai
                                        krôopkrua.
                                      ผม/ฉันต้องช่วยครอบครัว

◆ I will help you support your   pǒm/chán já chûai kun
    family.   sòng taang bâan.
                                      ผม/ฉันจะช่วยคุณส่งทางบ้าน

◆ I want to take you to America.   pǒm/chán yàak paa kun
                                        bpai a-mee-ri-kaa.
                                      ผม/ฉันอยากพาคุณไปอเมริกา

◆ My future depends on you.   a-naa-kót kǒong pǒm/chán
                                        kûn yùu gàp kun.
                                      อนาคตของผม/ฉันขึ้นอยู่กับคุณ

◆ I want to build my future   yàak jà sâang a-naa-kót
    with you.   gàp kun.
                                      อยากจะสร้างอนาคตกับคุณ

◆ I have _____.   pǒm/chán mii _____.
                                      ผม/ฉันมี _____

a son	lûuk chaai	ลูกชาย
a daughter	lûuk sǎao	ลูกสาว
a child	lûuk	ลูก
two children	lûuk sǒong kon	ลูกสองคน

◆ I have _____ but I wasn't married.

pŏm/chán mii _____ dtὲε mâi dâai dtὲng-ngaan.

ผม/ฉันมี _____ แต่ไม่ได้แต่งงาน

◆ I have _____ from a previous relationship.

pŏm/chán mii _____ gàp fεεn gào.

ผม/ฉันมี _____ กับแฟนเก่า

◆ I'll give you everything I have.

jà hâi kun túk yàang.

จะให้คุณทุกอย่าง

◆ We need to apply for a fiance visa.

rao dtông bpai kɔ̌ɔ wii-sâa kûu-mân.

เราต้องไปขอวีซ่าคู่หมั้น

◆ It's better to have the wedding in Thailand.

dtὲng-ngaan tîi mɯang tai dii gwàa.

แต่งงานที่เมืองไทยดีกว่า

◆ How much will the wedding cost?

jà chái kâa chái-jàai tâo-rài?

จะใช้ค่าใช้จ่ายเท่าไหร่?

◆ You have to pay a dowry.

kun jà dtông jàai kâa sĭnsɔ̀ɔt.

คุณจะต้องจ่ายค่าสินสอด

◆ The man pays for the dowry.

fàai chaai jàai kâa sĭnsɔ̀ɔt.

ฝ่ายชายจ่ายค่าสินสอด

◆ Do I have to pay a dowry?   dtôŋ hâi kâa sǐnsɔ̀ɔt mái?
                                          ต้องให้ค่าสินสอดมั้ย?

◆ How much should the dowry   kâa sǐnsɔ̀ɔt bpra-maan
     be?   tâo-rài?
                                          ค่าสินสอดประมาณเท่าไหร่?

◆ I don't care about the dowry.   mâi sǒnjai kâa sǐnsɔ̀ɔt.
                                          ฉันไม่สนใจค่าสินสอด

The Dowry

In Thailand it is traditional for the groom to pay the bride's family a dowry. What (generally cash) and how much is usually set at the engagement party. The dowry is supposed to be a gift to thank the parents of the bride for raising their daughter. As a practical matter much of it is used to cover the wedding expenses, since the bride's family generally takes responsibility for the wedding ceremony.

The amount of the dowry is determined by the social status of the bride's family, whether she has children or has been married before, her education and how pretty and desirable she is perceived to be. It also reflects on the groom's status (in case you haven't figured it out yet, status is largely a function of wealth) and can range from a few hundred dollars U.S. to many thousands. If you are going to take the bride away to live in a different country, don't be surprised if the quote for the dowry is quite high.

Traditional Thai weddings are expensive and many young people feel that they can't afford it. If the bride's family agrees, they may skip the dowry and split the expenses for a simple wedding. However, if you are a foreign man marrying a Thai woman, this is probably not the best course of action. As a foreigner who can travel internationally you are a person of some wealth by Thai standards— and therefore of at least moderately high status. To avoid paying a dowry under these circumstances could be perceived as an insult to the bride's family.

If you are a foreign woman marrying a Thai man, the dowry situation becomes one of negotiation between you and your fiance. Should you decide on a Thai wedding, the groom's family will probably be the ones to arrange it, in which case a dowry from the groom would seem to be double jeopardy! By the way, we have run across relatively few cases of foreign woman—Thai man marriages. For some reason the mutual attraction between Thai women and foreign men doesn't seem as widespread when the genders are reversed.

♦   You don't need to pay for the dowry.

kun mâi dtông sǐa kâa sǐnsòot.

คุณไม่ต้องเสียค่าสินสอด

♦   You just pay for the wedding.

kun sǐa dtὲε kâa jàt ngaan dtὲng-ngaan.

คุณเสียแต่ค่าจัดงานแต่งงาน

♦   We will have a traditional Thai wedding.

rao jà tam pí-tii bὲεp tai.

เราจะทำพิธีแบบไทย

♦   Let's get engaged first.

mân gan gòon dii gwàa.

หมั้นกันก่อนดีกว่า

♦   I will buy you a ring.

pǒm jà súu wěεn hâi kun.

ผมจะซื้อแหวนให้คุณ

◆ I'm so excited.   dtùun-dtên jang.
                                      ตื่นเต้นจัง

◆ International mariage is   dtèng-ngaan gàp kon
   difficult.   dtàang châat bpen rûang
                                         yâak.
                                      แต่งงานกับคนต่างชาติเป็นเรื่องยาก

◆ I think you'll be a good mother.   kít wâa kun jà bpen mÊÊ
                                         dii dii.
                                      คิดว่าคุณจะเป็นแม่ที่ดี

◆ I think you'll be a good father.   kít wâa kun jà bpen pÔÔ
                                         dii dii.
                                      คิดว่าคุณจะเป็นพ่อที่ดี

◆ I think we'll have a happy   kít wâa rao jà mii krÔÔp-
   family.   krua dii mii kwaam sùk.
                                      คิดว่าเราจะมีครอบครัวที่มีความสุข

◆ How many children do you   yàak mii lûuk gìi kon?
   want?   อยากมีลูกกี่คน?

Engagement and Wedding Ceremonies

An engagement party is usually held a few months prior to the wedding at the bride's house. It takes place in the morning and includes close relatives and friends of both the bride and groom. Engagement parties do not normally involve religious services. This is when the couple formally introduces themselves to each other's families. They also announce the terms of the dowry and date of the wedding. At the most auspicious moment the man places the engagement ring on his prospective bride's finger. Food and drinks are served afterwards.

Traditionally, the dates of the engagement party and wedding and the moment of placing the engagement ring on the woman's finger are determined by consulting with Buddhist monks. The monks refer to their astrological charts and determine the most auspicious times. Today, convenience often plays a larger role than astrology in determining the wedding day. Still, most Thais will not want to get married on a day that has been declared unlucky. After the big day is decided upon, the couple will print and send wedding invitations.

Thai weddings usually start early in the morning. Often the bride will begin preparing her hair and cosmetics at three or four in the morning. The actual ceremony starts with Buddhist monks chanting and blessing the bride and groom. Then food is served, with the monks eating first. After that the couple sits side by side, each wearing a headband joined by a white cord. Behind them stand the two best men and the two bridesmaids (all four should be unmarried). Meanwhile, the guests walk by and pour holy water on the hands of the bride and groom and wish them happiness, prosperity and long life. The wedding ceremony usually ends before noon and the bride and groom can rest until the evening reception. The reception is a time for food, drink, music, dancing and long-winded speeches extolling the virtues of the bride and groom. Wedding gifts are accepted in the form of money enclosed in an envelope with a card.

Thai weddings vary greatly according to the part of the country and preferences of the families, so the above description will not apply in many cases.

Useful Vocabulary

best man	pûan jâao-bàao เพื่อนเจ้าบ่าว
bride	jâao-sǎao เจ้าสาว
bridesmaid	pûan jâao-sǎao เพื่อนเจ้าสาว
Buddhism	sàatsa-nǎa pút ศาสนาพุทธ
Christianity	sàatsa-nǎa krít ศาสนาคริสต์
dowry	kâa sǐnsɔ̀ɔt ค่าสินสอด
engagement ceremony	pí-tii mân พิธีหมั้น
fiancé(e)	kûu-mân คู่หมั้น
friend	pûan เพื่อน
get engaged	mân หมั้น
groom	jâao-bàao เจ้าบ่าว
guest	kὲɛk แขก
Islam	sàtsa-nǎa ǐtsa-laam ศาสนาอิสลาม
marry	dtὲng-ngaan แต่งงาน
monk	prá พระ
relative	yâat ญาติ
religion	sàtsa-nǎa ศาสนา
style	bὲɛp, sa-taai แบบ, สไตล์
temple	wát วัด
wedding ceremony	pí-tii dtὲng-ngaan พิธีแต่งงาน
wedding ring	wěɛn dtὲng-ngaan แหวนแต่งงาน

See more kin terms in the appendix.

Women Marrying Up

In Thailand social status is very important when determining an acceptable marriage partner. Thailand has a large lower class, a substantial middle class and relatively small upper class elite. Social status is detemined by a variety of factors, among them education, family background, age and—perhaps most important—wealth. Although young lovers are increasingly more independent, family approval of the marriage is still extremely important to most Thai. In general, women are supposed to marry someone of equal or higher status. While it is certainly a factor, the groom's family is usually not as concerned about the social status of his mate and he can marry down without the same degree of family friction that his sisters would encounter. This creates a real numbers crunch for the middle class Thai woman. Many of her prospective mates have married down, thus depleting the pool of men available to her without a corresponding decrease in the number of single women within her social class. Also, middle class Thai men often don't feel any urgency to get married. Sex and companionship are easily available (see Chapter 9— "Nightlife"). Further muddying the marriage waters is the fact that Thai women often feel that Thai men, while they may be romantic and sweet, make poor husbands. They complain that men who can afford it have mistresses or "minor wives", visit brothels, gamble too much and drink. Whether true or false, such stereotypes tend to make middle class women cautious of men and marriage until they feel assured that these problems won't be an issue with their future husband. The above factors combine to create a very large pool of single, educated and attractive women who want to find a "good" husband. No doubt they have studied some English and can often communicate with foreigners fairly well. They may be teachers, secretaries, receptionists, college students, government workers or business women. Even if they come from a poor family, their education places them squarely in the middle class. All of the above should make Thailand a real happy hunting ground for single foreign men looking for a middle class, educated Thai wife. Unfortunately, this is not always the case. Breaking the social barriers that middle and upper class Thai woman put up may require an introduction by a trusted friend or a considerable period of time for her to evaluate you before you actually get to the dating stage. The effort may well be worth it. In our unscientific survey, these women often adapt more easily to an intercultural and international lifestyle than do those with less education.

To a woman from a poor family who has little education, a foreign husband could be a good catch— especially since her future prospects in Thailand are probably rather limited. Currently, she might be working as a hotel maid, waitress, unskilled laborer, farmer, retail sales clerk, etc. Or she may be one of the hundreds of thousands of girls working in the sex trade as masseuses, bar girls and prostitutes. Thai women are famous for their beauty and they often find Caucasian men attractive. Since the foreign man has the financial means to travel internationally, he obviously has some wealth and social status, and may offer a chance for financial improvement. This is important because most Thai women feel an obligation to help support their parents and other family members. Moving away from Thailand may seem either a frightening prospect or an opportunity, depending on the person.

CHAPTER EIGHT
Breaking Up

"Quarrels would not last long if the fault were only on one side."
—LA ROCHEFOUCAULD, *Maxims*

◆ I hate you.   pŏm/chán glìat kun.
                             ผม/ฉันเกลียดคุณ

◆ I'm tired of you.   pŏm/chán bùa kun.
                             ผม/ฉันเบื่อคุณ

◆ You are so boring.   kun nâa-bùa tîi-sùt.
                             คุณน่าเบื่อที่สุด

◆ I'm so bored with you.

pŏm/chán bùa kun mâak.

ผม/ฉันเบื่อคุณมาก

◆ It's all your fault.

túk yàang bpen kwaam
    pìt kŏong kun.

ทุกอย่างเป็นความผิดของคุณ

◆ Don't get me wrong.

yàa kâo-jai pìt.

อย่าเข้าใจผิด

◆ You nag too much.

kun bpen kon jûu-jîi mâak.

คุณเป็นคนจู้จี้มาก

◆ Stop complaining.

yùt bòn sá-tii.

หยุดบ่นซะที

◆ You are not my father.

kun mâi-châi pôo chán.

คุณไม่ใช่พ่อฉัน

◆ You are not my mother.

kun mâi-châi mêɛ pŏm.

คุณไม่ใช่แม่ผม

◆ Don't act like my father.

yàa maa tam dtua bpen pôo.

อย่ามาทำตัวเป็นพ่อ

◆ Don't act like my mother.

yàa maa tam dtua bpen mêɛ.

อย่ามาทำตัวเป็นแม่

◆ Don't act like a child.

yàa tam dtua mŭan dèk.

อย่าทำตัวเหมือนเด็ก

◆ You act like a child.

kun tam dtua mǔan dèk.
คุณทำตัวเหมือนเด็ก

◆ Why didn't you call me?

tammai mâi too maa?
ทำไมไม่โทรมา?

◆ You are so ugly.

kun nâa glìat mâak.
คุณน่าเกลียดมาก

◆ You are crazy.

kun man bâa.
คุณมันบ้า

◆ You are stupid!

ngîi-ngâo!
งี่เง่า!

◆ You make me so angry.

kun tam hâi pǒm/chán
    gròot mâak.
คุณทำให้ผม/ฉันโกรธมาก

◆ I love you, but I can't marry
  you.

pǒm/chán rák kun dtὲε
    dtὲng-ngaan dûai
    mâi-dâai.
ผม/ฉันรักคุณแต่แต่งงานด้วยไม่ได้

◆ I can't stand you anymore.

pǒm/chán ton kun mâi-dâai
    lέεo.
ผม/ฉันทนคุณไม่ได้แล้ว

◆ You hurt me so much.

kun tam hâi pŏm/chán
    jèp mâak.
คุณทำให้ผม/ฉันเจ็บมาก

◆ I'm so upset with you.

pŏm/chán pìtwǎng nai
    dtua kun mâak.
ผม/ฉันผิดหวังในตัวคุณมาก

◆ You broke my heart.

kun hàk òk pŏm/chán.
คุณหักอกผม/ฉัน

◆ Get out of here.

ɔ̀ɔk bpai jàak tîi-nîi.
ออกไปจากที่นี่

◆ Go away!

bpai hâi pón.
ไปให้พ้น

◆ Leave me alone.

yàak yùu kon diao.
อยากอยู่คนเดียว

◆ Don't touch me.

yàa maa tùuk dtua
    pŏm/chán.
อย่ามาถูกตัวผม/ฉัน

◆ I don't want to see you
    anymore.

mâi yàak hěn nâa kun ìik.
ไม่อยากเห็นหน้าคุณอีก

◆ I don't care about you anymore. mâi kɛɛ kun lɛ́ɛo.
ไม่แคร์คุณอีกแล้ว

◆ You cheated on me.   kun nɔ̂ɔk-jai pŏm/chán.
                                   คุณนอกใจผม/ฉัน

◆ You deceived me.   kun lɔ̀ɔk pŏm/chán.
                                   คุณหลอกผม/ฉัน

◆ You think that guy is better   kun kít-wâa pûu-chaai
    than me?   konnán dii gwàa pŏm
                                       châi-mái?
                                   คุณคิดว่าผู้ชายคนนั้นดีกว่า
                                       ผมใช่มั้ย?

◆ You think that girl is better   kun kít-wâa pûu-yĭng
    than me?   konnán dii gwàa chán
                                       châi-mái?
                                   คุณคิดว่าผู้หญิงคนนั้นดีกว่า
                                       ฉันใช่มั้ย?

◆ Somebody saw you go out   mii kon hěn kun bpai gàp
    with someone else.   kon ùɯn.
                                   มีคนเห็นคุณไปกับคนอื่น

◆ You slept with someone else.   kun nɔɔn gàp kon ùɯn.
                                   คุณนอนกับคนอื่น

◆ You are a two-timer.   kun man kon lăai jai.
                                   คุณมันคนหลายใจ

◆ You are promiscuous.   kun man kon săm-sɔ̀n.
                                   คุณมันคนสำส่อน

◆ You have many women.   kun mii pûu-yǐng lǎai kon.
                                  คุณมีผู้หญิงหลายคน

◆ You have many men.   kun mii pûu-chaai lǎai kon.
                                  คุณมีผู้ชายหลายคน

◆ You have a mistress.   kun mii mia nɔ́ɔi.
                                  คุณมีเมียน้อย

◆ I don't love you anymore.   pǒm/chán mâi rák kun lɛ́ɛo.
                                  ผม/ฉันไม่รักคุณแล้ว

◆ You don't trust me.   kun mâi-wâi-jai pǒm/chán.
                                  คุณไม่ไว้ใจผม/ฉัน

◆ I don't trust you anymore.   pǒm/chán mâi-wâi jai kun
                                      lɛ́ɛo.
                                  ผม/ฉันไม่ไว้ใจคุณแล้ว

◆ I'll look for someone else.   pǒm/chán jà hǎa kon mài.
                                  ผม/ฉันจะหาคนใหม่

◆ Go ahead and look for   chəən bpai hǎa kon mài.
      someone else.   เชิญไปหาคนใหม่

◆ I lied to you.   pǒm/chán goo-hòk kun.
                                  ผม/ฉันโกหกคุณ

◆ You lied to me.   kun goo-hòk pǒm/chán.
                                     คุณโกหกผม/ฉัน

◆ I'm sorry I lied to you.   kɔ̌ɔ-tôot fíi goo-hòk kun.
                                     ขอโทษที่โกหกคุณ

◆ You are such a liar.   kun kîi-goo-hòk.
                                     คุณขี้โกหก

◆ Liar.   kon goo-hòk.
                                     คนโกหก

◆ You have many secrets.   kun mii kwaam láp mâak.
                                     คุณมีความลับมาก

◆ Why didn't you tell me that   tammai kun mâi bɔ̀ɔk wâa
   you're already married?   dtɛ̀ng-ngaan lɛ́ɛo?
                                     ทำไมคุณไม่บอกว่าแต่งงานแล้ว?

◆ I never knew you had children.   mâi kəəi rúu wâa kun mii
                                        lûuk lɛ́ɛo.
                                     ไม่เคยรู้ว่าคุณมีลูกแล้ว

◆ I can't support your whole   pǒm/chán chûai krɔ̂ɔpkrua
   family.   kun tâng mòt mâi-dâai.
                                     ผม/ฉันช่วยครอบครัวคุณ
                                     ทั้งหมดไม่ได้

◆ I spent so much time and money on you.

pŏm/chán sĭa wee-laạ lé ngən gàp kun bpai mâak.

ผม/ฉันเสียเวลาและเงิน
กับคุณไปมาก

◆ You acted like you had money.

kun tam dtua mŭan kon mii ngən.

คุณทำตัวเหมือนคนมีเงิน

◆ I shouldn't have wasted time on you.

mâi-nâa sĭa wee-laa gàp kun ləəi.

ไม่น่าเสียเวลากับคุณเลย

◆ You love my money, not me.

kun rák ngən kɔ̌ɔng pŏm/chán, mâi-dâai rák dtua pŏm/chán.

คุณรักเงินของผม/ฉัน
ไม่ได้รักตัวผม/ฉัน

◆ I don't want to see your face anymore.

mâi-yàak hěn nâa kun ĭik.

ไม่อยากเห็นหน้าคุณอีก

◆ I'm hurt enough.

pŏm/chán jèp pɔɔ lέεo.

ผม/ฉันเจ็บพอแล้ว

◆ I don't want to shed any tears for you.

mâi-yàak sĭa náam-dtaa hâi kun.

ไม่อยากเสียน้ำตาให้คุณ

◆ I'm not going to cry.   pŏm/chán jà mâi róɔng-hâi.
                                            ผม/ฉันจะไม่ร้องไห้

◆ We should break up.   rao kuan lɔ̂ɔk gan.
                                            เราควรเลิกกัน

◆ It's better that we break up.   lɔ̂ɔk gan dii gwàa.
                                            เลิกกันดีกว่า

◆ I'm the one who is wrong.   pŏm/chán bpen kon pìt.
                                            ผม/ฉันเป็นคนผิด

◆ I'm sorry for the things I've   pŏm/chán sĭa-jai gàp sĭng
   done.   tîi tam bpai.
                                            ผม/ฉันเสียใจกับสิ่งที่ทำไป

◆ Please forgive me.   yók-tôot hâi pŏm/chán dûai.
                                            ยกโทษให้ผม/ฉันด้วย

◆ I forgive you.   pŏm/chán yók-tôot hâi kun.
                                            ผม/ฉันยกโทษให้คุณ

◆ I can't forgive you.   yók-tôot hâi kun mâi-dâai.
                                            ยกโทษให้คุณไม่ได้

◆ Too bad we don't get along.   sĭa-daai tîi rao bpai dûai
                                                gan mâi-dâai.
                                            เสียดายที่เราไปด้วยกันไม่ได้

◆ You'll find someone else soon. kun jà hăa kon mài dâai
                                        reo-reo níi.
                                    คุณจะหาคนใหม่ได้เร็วๆ นี้

◆ Go ahead and find another   kun bpai mii kon mài dâai.
  lover.   คุณไปมีคนใหม่ได้

◆ You can find someone better.   kun hăa kon tîi dii gwàa
                                        dâai.
                                    คุณหาคนที่ดีกว่าได้

◆ You gave me a good   kun sŏɔn bpra-sòp gaan
  experience.   tîi-dii hâi pŏm/chán.
                                    คุณสอนประสบการณ์ที่ดี
                                        ให้ผม/ฉัน

◆ I still want to be friends   pŏm/chán yang yàak jà
  with you.   bpen pûan gàp kun.
                                    ผม/ฉันยังอยากจะเป็นเพื่อนกับคุณ

◆ But I don't want to see you   dtɛ̀ɛ pŏm/chán mâi-yàak
  anymore.   hĕn kun ĭik.
                                    แต่ผม/ฉันไม่อยากเห็นคุณอีก

◆ Don't call me anymore.   yàa too maa-hăa ĭik.
                                    อย่าโทรมาหาอีก

◆ Let's get a divorce.   yàa gan dii gwàa.
                                    หย่ากันดีกว่า

◆ I want to divorce you.

pŏm/chán dtɔ̂ng-gaan yàa
gàp kun.
ผม/ฉันต้องการหย่ากับคุณ

◆ I'll try to forget you.

jà pa-yaa-yaam lʉʉm kun.
จะพยายามลืมคุณ

◆ You will still be in my heart.

kun jà yang yùu nai hŭa-jai
kɔ̌ɔng pŏm/chán.
คุณจะยังอยู่ในหัวใจของผม/ฉัน

◆ We can still be friends.

rao yang bpen pʉ̂an gan
dâai.
เรายังเป็นเพื่อนกันได้

◆ I don't want to be friends
anymore.

mâi yàak bpen pʉ̂an ʼiik
dtɔ̀ɔ bpai.
ไม่อยากเป็นเพื่อนอีกต่อไป

◆ Don't contact me.

yàa dtìt-dtɔ̀ɔ maa.
อย่าติดต่อมา

◆ I don't want to see your
face anymore.

mâi yàak hĕn nâa kun ʼiik.
ไม่อยากเห็นหน้าคุณอีก

◆ I don't want you to
contact me.

mâi-yàak hâi kun dtìt-dtɔ̀ɔ
maa.
ไม่อยากให้คุณติดต่อมา

◆ I will return all your stuff.   jà kʉʉn kɔ̌ɔng túk yàang
                                     hâi kun.
                                     จะคืนของทุกอย่างให้คุณ

◆ I'm glad we ended it.   dii jai tîi rao lə̂ək gan.
                                     ดีใจที่เราเลิกกัน

◆ Let's end it on good terms.   lə̂ək gan dii-dii dii-gwàa.
                                     เลิกกันดีๆ ดีกว่า

◆ Good luck with your new love.   kɔ̌ɔ hâi chôok dii gàp
                                     rák mài.
                                     ขอให้โชคดีกับรักใหม่

CHAPTER NINE
Night Life

"Give me chastity and continence—but not yet."
—SAINT AUGUSTINE, *Confessions*

Much of the nightlife in Thailand is male oriented and revolves around ladies of easy virtue, but Thai people are a fun loving group as a whole and your Thai partner will probably be glad to offer suggestions for a respectable night time outing. Bangkok, in particular, has a wide range of venues for an entertaining evening. If you like live music, check out the row of nightclubs near Lumpini Park. For the dance crowd, Bangkok has some of the largest discoteques in Asia. If your taste runs more to ballroom, you could try the Galaxy, where waltz, swing and cha-cha are the order of the night.

Most Thai people love to sing and Karaoke bars have become very popular, with many establishments having extensive song selections in Thai, English and Japanese. Private rooms are often available. Prices are extremely reasonable by international standards.

Movies are also a good choice— most towns in Thailand have a theatre. Foreign films are common so you may find yourself watching a movie in English while your date reads the Thai subtitles.

The real staple of a Thai night out, though, is dinner. Bangkok excels in this regard with the world's largest restaurant (the waiters wear roller skates), dinner cruises on the Chao Phraya river and classical dance floor shows. Good restaurants abound throughout the rest of Thailand as well.

Love for Sale

An unaccompanied foreign man in Thailand can hardly avoid the sex industry. Whether he chooses to participate or not is, of course, up to him. There are brothels in virtually every town— just ask any taxi driver. Not to mention the numerous massage parlors, go-go bars, cocktail lounges, private men's clubs, beer gardens and coffee shops which offer intimate female companionship. Because of the huge sex business with foreigners, people often conclude that Thailand has been corrupted by foreign money and that prostitution is a recent perversion of Thai culture. This is not entirely the case. Certainly Thailand's status as an R & R destination and host of U.S. bases during the Vietnam war and the seemingly endless flood of male tourists looking for cheap sex have boosted the industry, but Thailand had a very active sex trade before the foreign influx.

Most prostitutes come from the lower class economically and educationally. Although their earnings may be quite high, they pay a price in status. Prostitutes are at the bottom of the social ladder. To the village girl working in Bangkok this may not matter so much. After all, she doesn't really care what people in Bangkok think and she doesn't have to tell anyone back in the village exactly what she does. As long as she is sending money home they will probably not be too nosey. When she returns, with the money she has earned, she can create a better life for herself and her family and perhaps buy some land or a business.

Maybe she'll even get lucky and find a rich foreigner to marry. This happens quite frequently— often with false expectations on both sides. The foreign man turns out not to be as rich as he seemed or perhaps doesn't give her as much access to his money as she would like. The workaday life in his country is very different from the time they spent together while he was on vacation in Thailand and the language and cultural differences are a challenge. From the man's perspective, he may believe that he is saving her from a terrible life and that she will show her gratitude by being a loving and faithful wife. He forgets that her lifestyle has been one in which love and affection are sold for cash. When her priority turns out to be sending money home to her family back in Thailand instead of creating a new life with him, he feels betrayed.

The above dismal scenario is by no means true of all couples. Some former ladies of the night turn out to adapt quite well to life abroad and end up having mutually rewarding marriages with their foreign spouses.

Following are some of the more common settings where sex is for sale:

Massage Parlors

There is traditional Thai therapeutic message in which sex plays no part, but here we are talking about the more erotic variety usually called àap òp nûat (bath and massage). The parlors range from small establishments with a few girls to glitzy, neon lit places the size of a Macy's department store. As you walk into the lobby you will usually see a glass wall with women sitting behind it. Each one wears a small number badge. When you pick the masseuse you want, tell the parlor employee her number. Often you will be asked whether you want massage only or wish to pay extra for full service. Full service includes sex. Your masseuse will come out and retrieve you and take you to a massage room. You take a bath together and she gives you a massage and, if you paid for it, sex. If not, she will probably try to negotiate an additional tip in exchange for sexual services.

Brothels and Escort Services

Often tucked out of the way on a back street, brothels are most easily found by asking a taxi driver. Once there, you can pick a girl from a lineup.

Escort services will send a girl to your hotel. Their telephone numbers are often advertised in the English language newspapers.

Go-go Bars and Cocktail Lounges

Go-go bars are usually clustered together in tourist areas and cater primarily to foreigners. Patpong Street in Bangkok is probably the most famous concentration of bars in Thailand but there are many others. Generally, go-go bars have a stage where bikini clad girls dance. Like massage girls, they wear identifying badges with numbers.

The upstairs bars on Patpong offer sex shows and the dancers often dispense with bikinis entirely. Be sure to clarify the policy on cover charges. Many establishments have none at all, but others have been known to surprise customers with a larger than expected bill including a hefty cover charge.

In between dance shifts, the bar girls socialize with customers. If you would like to talk to one, buy her a "lady drink" (usually a small Coca-Cola since the girls aren't allowed to drink alcohol while working) and she will sit with you for a while. If you want more intimate relations, you can pay the bar a commission, called a bar fine, for either "short time" or all night. Some bars have short time rooms right on the premises. If you payed for all night, where you go and what you do is negotiable between you and the girl. A key point to remember is that the bar fine is only for the bar—you still have to negotiate a fee with the girl.

Bar girls usually have some discretion over who they go with and what they do. If a girl doesn't like you, she may refuse to be bar fined. Of course, if this happens repeatedly with various customers, she probably won't be popular with the bar management.

Many cocktail lounges have hostesses that can be hired by the hour to sit and keep you company. They can be taken out as well. The arrangement is similar to go-go bars.

Private Men's Clubs

Wealthy Thai businessmen often belong to one or more men's clubs. They can entertain their business associates there or just relax with friends. Some of these clubs are virtual palaces of oppulence with live entertainment and a large staff of girls available to the members and guests. Membership in the better clubs is expensive and for a longer term than suits most tourists.

Beer Gardens and Coffee Shops

Freelance prostitutes frequent these places. There is no cover charge and they can nurse a cup of coffee or a beer for hours while waiting to get picked up.

In Bangkok, the Thermae Coffee Shop on Sukhumvit Road near Soi 13 is well known. It stays open after the bars close, so bar girls who were unsuccessful in getting bar fined out for the night often go there after work to drum up some additional business. By 2 or 3 o'clock in the morning the Thermae is really hopping. Since the coffee shop is not directly involved with prostitution (it just sells coffee and beer to everyone), everything is negotiable between you and the girl.

AIDS and other STDs

AIDS and other sexually transmitted deseases have reached epidemic proportions in Thailand. While many STDs involve a trip to a clinic and a few shots or pills, there is still no cure for AIDS. PRACTICE SAFE SEX! Use a condom and make sure you use it correctly.

Here are some sentences for your night life outings. Chapters 3, 4 and 5 also have some useful phrases.

◆   I want to have a massage.   yàak bpai nûat.
                                         อยากไปนวด

◆   I want to have a traditional   yàak bpai nûat pĕɛn
     Thai massage.   boo-raan.
                                         อยากไปนวดแผนโบราณ

◆ Where is a good massage
  parlor?

mii ĝii nuàt năi dii bâang?
มีที่นวดไหนบ้าง?

◆ I want to go to a disco.

yàak bpai dítsa-gôo.
อยากไปดิสโก้

◆ Do you know a good disco?

rúu-jàk dítsa-gôo-tèk dii-dii
    bâang mái?
รู้จักดิสโก้เทคดีๆ บ้างมั้ย?

◆ Which bar is the best?

baa năi dii ĝii-sùt?
บาร์ไหนดีที่สุด?

◆ Taxi, take me to Patpong.

téksîi, paa-bpai pátpong nòi.
แท็กซี่ พาไปพัฒน์พงษ์หน่อย

◆ There is a _____ close by.

mii _____ yùu glâi-glâi.
มี _____ อยู่ใกล้ๆ

  bar
  gay bar
  discotheque
  massage parlor
  traditional Thai massage

baa บาร์
baa-gee บาร์เกย์
dítsa-gôo-tèk ดิสโก้เทค
àap-òp-nûat อาบอบนวด
nûat pĕɛn boo-raan
    นวดแผนโบราณ

◆ Is there a _____ close by?

mii _____ yùu glâi-glâi mái?
มี _____ อยู่ใกล้ๆ มั้ย?

◆   Which is the best bar?   baa-nǎi dii ʨii-sùt?
                                          บาร์ไหนดีที่สุด

◆   This is the best bar.   baa-níi dii ʨii-sùt.
                                          บาร์นี้ดีที่สุด

◆   I want to visit a gay bar.   yàak bpai duu baa-gee.
                                          อยากไปดูบาร์เกย์

◆   I think that fellow is gay.   kít wâa kon nán bpen gee.
                                          คิดว่าคนนั้นเป็นเกย์

◆   Do you often come here?   kun maa ʨii-níi bɔ̀i mái?
                                          คุณมาที่นี่บ่อยไหม?

    ●   Very often.   bɔ̀i mâak.
                                          บ่อยมาก

    ●   Sometimes.   baang kráng.
                                          บางครั้ง

    ●   This is my first time.   maa kráng-rɛ̂ɛk.
                                          มาครั้งแรก

◆   Do you smoke?   kun sùup bu-rǐi mái?
                                          คุณสูบบุหรี่ไหม?

◆   Do you drink alcohol?   kun gin lâo mái?
                                          คุณกินเหล้าไหม?

◆   Do you like working here?   kun chɔ̂ɔp tam-ngaan ʨii-níi
                                              rú-bplàao?
                                          คุณชอบทำงานที่นี่รึเปล่า?

- Very much.

  chɔ̂ɔp mâak.

  ชอบมาก

- I don't like it at all.

  mâi chɔ̂ɔp ləəi.

  ไม่ชอบเลย

- I don't like it, but I have to.

  mâi chɔ̂ɔp dtɛ̀ɛ dtɔ̂ng tam.

  ไม่ชอบแต่ต้องทำ

◆ How long have you been
  working here?

  kun tam-ngaan tîi-nîi naan
      tâo-rài lɛ́ɛo?

  คุณทำงานที่นี่นานเท่าไหร่แล้ว?

- Not so long.

  mâi naan tâo-rài.

  ไม่นานเท่าไหร่

- About a year.

  bpra-maan nùng bpii.

  ประมาณหนึ่งปี

◆ How many hours do you work
  a night?

  kun tam-ngaan kʉʉn lá
      gìi chûa-mong?

  คุณทำงานคืนละกี่ชั่วโมง?

- From 8 pm to 2 am.

  jàak sɔ̌ɔng tûm tǔng
      dtii sɔ̌ɔng.

  จากสองทุ่มถึงตีสอง

◆ Do you like being a dancer?

  kun chɔ̂ɔp dtên rʉ́-bplàao?

  คุณชอบเต้นหรือเปล่า?

- Not so much.

  mâi kɔ̂i chɔ̂ɔp.

  ไม่ค่อยชอบ

- I think it's a fun job.

  kítwâa bpen ngaan tîi
      sa-nùk.

  คิดว่าเป็นงานที่สนุก

● It's very boring.

nâa-bùa mâak.
น่าเบื่อมาก

◆ I want to dance with you.

yàak dtên ram gàp kun.
อยากเต้นรำกับคุณ

◆ Do you like this work?

kun chɔ̂ɔp ngaan níi mái?
คุณชอบงานนี้มั้ย?

◆ I like this work.

chɔ̂ɔp ngaan níi.
ชอบงานนี้

◆ I hate this work.

mâi chɔ̂ɔp ngaan níi.
ไม่ชอบงานนี้

◆ It's an easy way to make money.

ngaan níi hǎa ngən ngâi.
งานนี้หาเงินง่าย

◆ I like to have fun.

pǒm/chán chɔ̂ɔp sa-nùk.
ผม/ฉันชอบสนุก

◆ I don't know what work to do.

mâi rúu jà tam-ngaan a-rai.
ไม่รู้จะทำงานอะไร

◆ I have little education.

pǒm/chán mâi kɔ̂i mii
     kwaam-rúu.
ผม/ฉันไม่ค่อยมีความรู้

◆ I want to quit this job.

yàak jà lə̂ək tam-ngaan níi.
อยากจะเลิกทำงานนี้

◆ Where did you learn
   massage?

   ● At Wat Pho (a temple).

kun rian nûat fii-nǎi?

คุณเรียนนวดที่ไหน

fii wát-poo.

ที่วัดโพธิ์

◆ I haven't eaten anything.

yang mâi-dâai gin a-rai
   ləəi.

ยังไม่ได้กินอะไรเลย

◆ May I order you something?

pǒm/chán jà sàng a-rai hâi
   ao-mái?

ผม/ฉันจะสั่งอะไรให้เอาไหม?

◆ May I buy you a drink?

pǒm/chán jà sàng krûang
   dùum hâi ao-mái?

ผม/ฉันจะสั่งเครื่องดื่มให้เอาไหม?

◆ What would you like to drink?

yàak dùum a-rai?

อยากดื่มอะไร?

◆ Drink a little more.

dùum ìik nɔ̀i.

ดื่มอีกหน่อย

◆ You are drunk.

kun mao lɛ́ɛo.

คุณเมาแล้ว

◆ I'm not drunk.

pǒm/chán mâi mao.

ผม/ฉันไม่เมา

◆ I want to go out with you.   yàak ɔ̀ɔk bpai kâang-nɔ̂ɔk
                                        gàp kun.
                                      อยากออกไปข้างนอกกับคุณ

◆ I want to take you out.   yàak paa kun ɔ̀ɔk bpai.
                                      อยากพาคุณออกไป

◆ Please take me out.   paa pǒm/chán ɔ̀ɔk bpai nɔ̀i.
                                      พาผม/ฉันออกไปหน่อย

◆ How can I take you out?   jà paa bpai dâai yang-ngai?
                                      จะพาไปได้ยังไง?

◆ You have to pay the bar.   kun jàai ngən hâi gàp baa.
                                      คุณจ่ายเงินให้กับบาร์

◆ This is a tip for you.   níi típ kɔ̌ɔng kun.
                                      นี่ทิปของคุณ

◆ Tonight isn't a good night.   kɯɯn-níi mâi sa-dùak.
                                      คืนนี้ไม่สะดวก

◆ I will come again tomorrow.   prûng-níi jà maa ìik.
                                      พรุ่งนี้จะมาอีก

◆ I will wait for you.   pǒm/chán jà rɔɔ kun.
                                      ผม/ฉันจะรอคุณ

◆ I want to be with you tonight.　kʉʉn-níi yàak yùu gàp kun.
คืนนี้อยากอยู่กับคุณ

◆ Do you want to sleep with me?　yàak nɔɔn gàp pǒm/chán mái?
อยากนอนกับผม/ ฉันมั้ย?

◆ I will take you to my hotel.　jà paa kun bpai roong-rɛɛm.
จะพาคุณไปโรงแรม

◆ Do you want short time
　or overnight?　kun dtɔ̂ng-gaan chûa-kraao rʉ̌ʉ káang-kʉʉn?
คุณต้องการชั่วคราวหรือค้างคืน?

◆ How much do you charge?　kun kít tâo-rài?
คุณคิดเท่าไหร่?

◆ How much do you charge
　per night?　kun kít kâa káang-kʉʉn tâo-rài?
คุณคิดค่าค้างคืนเท่าไหร่?

◆ How much do you charge
　for short time?　kun kít kâa chûa-kraao tâo-rài?
คุณคิดค่าชั่วคราวเท่าไหร่?

◆ That's very expensive.　pɛɛng mâak.
แพงมาก

◆ Can you make it lower?   lótnɔ̀i dâai mái?
                                      ลดหน่อยได้มั้ย

◆ That's a standard price.   raa-kaa mâat-dta-tăan.
                                      ราคามาตรฐาน

◆ Let's go to a different bar.   bpai baa ừừn dii-gwàa.
                                      ไปบาร์อื่นดีกว่า

◆ There is a good coffee shop   mii kɔ́-fii-chɔ̀p tîi nâa-sŏn
   near Soi 13.   jai yùu sɔɔi sìp săam.
                                      มีคอฟฟี่ช็อพที่น่าสนใจอยู่ซอยสิบสาม

◆ I like to go there after work.   pŏm/chán chɔ̂ɔp bpai tîi-
                                         nân lăng lôək ngaan.
                                      ผม/ฉันชอบไปที่นั่นหลังเลิกงาน

◆ There are lots of people there   mii kon bpai mâak lăng
   after midnight.   tîang-kừừn.
                                      มีคนไปมากหลังเที่ยงคืน

◆ A lot of girls wait there to   pûak pûu-yĭng kɔɔi póp
   meet foreigners.   kὲεk dtàang bpra-têet.
                                      พวกผู้หญิงคอยพบแขกต่างประเทศ

◆ I like that place.   pŏm/chán chɔ̂ɔp tîi-nân.
                                      ผม/ฉันชอบที่นั่น

◆   I don't like that place.

pǒm/chán mâi chɔ̂ɔp
   tii-nân.
ผม/ฉันไม่ชอบที่นั่น

◆   It's too smoky.

měn bu-rìi.
เหม็นบุหรี่

◆   It's late.

dùk lέεo.
ดึกแล้ว

◆   I'm sleepy.

ngûang-nɔɔn.
ง่วงนอน

◆   I want to go home.

yàak glàp bâan.
อยากกลับบ้าน

◆   I'd better go home.

glàp bâan dii gwàa.
กลับบ้านดีกว่า

◆   I'm going back to my hotel.

jà glàp roong-rεεm.
จะกลับโรงแรม

◆   Come see me here again.

maa-hǎa pǒm/chán ʔik ná.
มาหาผม/ฉันที่นี่อีกนะ

◆   Don't forget to come see me.

yàa luum maa-hǎa
   pǒm/chán ná.
อย่าลืมมาหาผม/ฉันนะ

◆ I promise to come back.   pŏm/chán săn-yaa wâa
                                    jà glàp maa ìik.
                                    ผม/ฉันสัญญาว่าจะกลับมาอีก

◆ Hope to see you soon.   wăng wâa jà dâai jəə kun
                                    ìik reo-reo níi.
                                    หวังว่าจะได้เจออีกเร็วๆ นี้

Slang and Colloquialisms

The following slang expressions are commonly used
among close friends and young people. Thai people will be surprised to hear these words from a foreigner. Don't forget that
you should use them with close friends only.

bad (something)	hùai ห่วย
bisexual	bai ไบ
broke (no money)	tăng-dtèɛk ถังแตก
cool (young people)	jáap จ๊าบ
delicious	sâp แซ่บ
drag king	tɔm ทอม
drag queen	dîi ดี้
easy women	gài ไก่
excrement (dung)	kîi ขี้
exhausted	dîang เดี้ยง
fail	hêo แห้ว
fart	dtòt ตด
feces	ìì อี, kîi ขี้
hang-over	mao-káang เมาค้าง
have an affair	mii-chúu มีชู้
gay queen	dtút ตุ๊ด
	dtěo แต๋ว

	ii-èɛp อีแอบ
	bpra-tʉang ประเทือง
	ga-təəi กะเทย
in the closet gay	èɛpjìt แอบจิต
to look for easy women	jàp gài จับไก่
go pee (urinate)	bpai-chìi, bpai-chíng-chɔ̀ng ไปฉี่, ไปฉิ้งฉ่อง
go pee (men only)	ying-gra-dtàai ยิงกระต่าย
masturbate (men)	chák-wâao ชักว่าว
masturbate (women)	dtòk-bèt ตกเบ็ด
modern (people)	sîng ซิ่ง
old maid	sǎao kʉ̂nkaan สาวขึ้นคาน
penis	nók-kǎo นกเขา
perfect	níap เนี้ยบ
perform a blow job	móok โม้ก
pimp	mɛɛng-daa แมงดา
pretend not to know	tamgǎi ทำไก๋
pretentious	dàtja-rìt ดัดจริต
pussy	jǐm จิ๋ม
rented wife	mia-châo เมียเช่า
sad	jɔ̌i จ๋อย
saucy	ta-lʉ̂ng ทะลึ่ง
semen	náam rák น้ำรัก
smart (looking)	têe เท่
smelly fart	dtòtměn ตดเหม็น
stingy (cheap)	kîi-dtʉ̀ʉt ขี้ตืด
unlucky	suai ซวย
woman (gay calling women)	cha-nii ชะนี
wonderful	jɛ̌ɛo แจ๋ว

Profanity

The following words are taboo. **Never** use them in public— they could really get you into big trouble. These words will offend most Thai people that hear them.

ass	dàak
asshole	ruu-dàak
bad mouth	bpàakmǎa
bitch	nâa-dtua-mia
butt in	sùak
clitoris	dtèɛt
despicable	hîa, ra-yam
fuck	yét
fuckable	nâa-yét
he/she/they	man
I	guu
move penis in and out	dâo
penis (little boy)	jǔu, jíao
penis	kuai
prostitute (female)	ii-dtua, ga-rìi
prostitute (male)	âi-dtua
pubic hair	mɔ̌ɔi
slut	ii-dɔ̀ɔk
take each other	ao-gan
testicles	hǎm, kài-hǎm
you	mʉng
you animal	âi-sàt
vagina	hǐi
withered penis	hǎm hìao
withered pussy	hǐi hìao

APPENDIX

Quick References

APPENDIX
Quick Reference

This is only a quick reference for your convenience. If you would like to have a more detailed word list and usage guidelines, please see "Thai for Beginners" and "Thai for Intermediate Learners".

Numbers

0	sǔun	ศูนย์
1	nùng	หนึ่ง
2	sɔ̌ɔng	สอง
3	sǎam	สาม
4	sìi	สี่
5	hâa	ห้า
6	hòk	หก
7	jèt	เจ็ด
8	bpὲɛt	แปด
9	gâao	เก้า
10	sìp	สิบ
11	sìp-èt	สิบเอ็ด
12	sìpsɔ̌ɔng	สิบสอง
13	sìpsǎam	สิบสาม
20	yîi-sìp	ยี่สิบ
21	yîi-sìp-èt	ยี่สิบเอ็ด
22	yîi-sìpsɔ̌ɔng	ยี่สิบสอง
30	sǎamsìp	สามสิบ
31	sǎamsìp-èt	สามสิบเอ็ด

32	săamsìpsɔ̌ɔng	สามสิบสอง
40	sìi-sìp	สี่สิบ
50	hâa-sìp	ห้าสิบ
60	hòksìp	หกสิบ
70	jètsìp	เจ็ดสิบ
80	bpὲɛtsìp	แปดสิบ
90	gâao-sìp	เก้าสิบ
100	(nùng) rɔ́ɔi	(หนึ่ง) ร้อย
200	sɔ̌ɔngrɔ́ɔi	สองร้อย
300	săamrɔ́ɔi	สามร้อย
1,000	(nùng) pan	(หนึ่ง) พัน
2,000	sɔ̌ɔngpan	สองพัน
3,000	săampan	สามพัน
10,000	(nùng) mɨ̀ɨn	(หนึ่ง) หมื่น
100,000	(nùng) sɛ̌ɛn	(หนึ่ง) แสน
1,000,000	(nùng) láan	(หนึ่ง) ล้าน
10,000,000	sìp láan	สิบล้าน
100,000,000	(nùng) rɔ́ɔi láan	(หนึ่ง) ร้อยล้าน
1,000,000,000	(nùng) pan láan	(หนึ่ง) พันล้าน
10,000,000,000	(nùng) mɨ̀ɨn láan	(หนึ่ง) หมื่นล้าน
100,000,000,000	(nùng) sɛ̌ɛn láan	(หนึ่ง) แสนล้าน
1,000,000,000,000	(nùng) láan láan	(หนึ่ง) ล้านล้าน

Summary of the Thai Writng System

The 44 Thai Consonants in
Alphabetical Order

Consonant	Consonant Name	Sound
ก	ก ไก่ gɔɔ gài *(chicken)*❀	/g/
ข	ข ไข่ kɔ̌ɔ kài *(egg)*❖	/k/
ฃ	ฃ ขวด kɔ̌ɔ kùat *(bottle)*❖	/k/
ค	ค ควาย kɔɔ kwaai *(buffalo)*	/k/
ฅ	ฅ คน kɔɔ kon *(person)*	/k/
ฆ	ฆ ระฆัง kɔɔ rá-kang *(bell)*	/k/
ง	ง งู ngɔɔ nguu *(snake)*	/ng/
จ	จ จาน jɔɔ jaan *(plate)*❀	/j/
ฉ	ฉ ฉิ่ง chɔ̌ɔ chìng *(small cymbal)*❖	/ch/
ช	ช ช้าง chɔɔ cháang *(elephant)*	/ch/

ซ	ซ โซ่	sɔɔ sôo *(chain)*	/s/
ฌ	ฌ เฌอ	chɔɔ chəə *(a kind of tree)*	/ch/
ญ	ญ หญิง	yɔɔ yǐng *(woman)*	/y/
ฎ	ฎ ชะฎา	dɔɔ chá-daa *(a kind of crown)*✿	/d/
ฏ	ฏ ปะฏัก	dtɔɔ bpà-dtàk *(a kind of spear)*✿	/dt/
ฐ	ฐ ฐาน	tɔɔ tǎan *(base)*❖	/t/
ฑ	มณโฑ	tɔɔ montoo *(Montho the Queen)*	/t/
ฒ	ฒ ผู้เฒ่า	tɔɔ pûu-tâo *(old man)*	/t/
ณ	ณ เณร	nɔɔ neen *(young monk)*	/n/
ด	ด เด็ก	dɔɔ dèk *(child)*✿	/d/
ต	ต เต่า	dtɔɔ dtào *(turtle)*✿	/dt/
ถ	ถ ถุง	tɔɔ tǔng *(bag)*❖	/t/
ท	ท ทหาร	tɔɔ tá-hǎan *(soldier)*	/t/
ธ	ธ ธง	tɔɔ tong *(flag)*	/t/

น	น หนู	nɔɔ nŭu *(mouse)*	/n/
บ	บ ใบไม้	bɔɔ bai-máai *(leaf)*✿	/b/
ป	ป ปลา	bpɔɔ bplaa *(fish)*✿	/bp/
ผ	ผ ผึ้ง	pɔɔ pûng *(bee)*❖	/p/
ฝ	ฝ ฝา	fɔɔ făa *(lid)*❖	/f/
พ	พ พาน	pɔɔ paan *(tray)*	/p/
ฟ	ฟ ฟัน	fɔɔ fan *(tooth)*	/f/
ภ	ภ สำเภา	pɔɔ sămpao *(a kind of ship)*	/p/
ม	ม ม้า	mɔɔ máa *(horse)*	/m/
ย	ย ยักษ์	yɔɔ yák *(giant)*	/y/
ร	ร เรือ	rɔɔ rɰa (boat)	/r/
ล	ล ลิง	lɔɔ ling *(monkey)*	/l/
ว	ว แหวน	wɔɔ wɛ̆ɛn *(ring)*	/w/
ศ	ศ ศาลา	sɔɔ săa-laa *(pavilion)*❖	/s/

ษ	ษ ฤๅษี	sɔ̌ɔ rɯɯ-sǐi *(hermit)*❖	/s/
ส	ส เสือ	sɔ̌ɔ sǔa *(tiger)*❖	/s/
ห	ห หีบ	hɔ̌ɔ hìip *(a kind of box)*❖	/h/
ฬ	ฬ จุฬา	lɔɔ jù-laa *(a kind of kite)*	/l/
อ	อ อ่าง	ɔɔ àang *(basin)*✿	/ɔ/
ฮ	ฮ นกฮูก	hɔɔ nókhûuk (owl)	/h/

❖   = high consonant (11 out of 44)
✿   = middle consonant (9 out of 44)
No mark   = low consonant (24 out of 44)

Note: Every Thai consonant has a name which distiguishes it
       from other consonants with the same sound. Since these
       names are standardized and universal, you can always tell
       Thai people how to spell a word without having to
       actually show them.

Vowels (sàrà - สระ)

1. –ะ /à/   –า /aa/

2. –ิ /ĭ/   –ี /ii/

3. –ึ /ǔ/   –ื่อ /ʉʉ/

4. –ุ /ù/   –ู /uu/

5. เ–ะ /è/   เ– /ee/

6. แ–ะ /ɛ̀/   แ– /ɛɛ/

7. โ–ะ /ò/   โ– /oo/

8. เ–าะ /ɔ̀/   –อ /ɔɔ/

9. –ัวะ /ùa/   –ัว /ua/

10. เ–ียะ /ĭa/   เ–ีย /ia/

11. เ–ือะ /ǔa/   เ–ือ /ʉa/

12. เ–อะ /ə̀/   เ–อ /əə/

Note: 1-12 on the left are short vowels and their counterparts
(long vowels) are on the right.

Some of the following vowels may sound either short or long, but they are categorized as long vowels for tone rule purposes.

ำ (am)

ไ- (ai mái-múan)

ใ- (ai mái-má-lai)

เ-า (ao)

เ-ย (əəi)

Tone Marks

Thai has four tone marks.

Tone Mark	Name
ı	
—	mái èek (ไม้เอก)
◡	
—	mái too (ไม้โท)
◯	
— +	mái dtrii (ไม้ตรี)
—	mái jàt-dtà-waa (ไม้จัตวา)

'mái' (ไม้) refers to the tone mark, not to the tone sound of the syllable in which it occurs. 'mái dtrii' and 'mái jàt-dtà-waa' can be used with middle consonants only.

Tone Names

Many Thai syllables have no tone mark at all. Every syllable in Thai is pronounced with one of the five tones, however, and each of these tone sounds has a name as follows:

Tone	Tone Name	
Mid Tone	sǐang sǎa-man	(เสียงสามัญ)
Low Tone	sǐang èek	(เสียงเอก)
Falling Tone	sǐang too	(เสียงโท)
High Tone	sǐang dtrii	(เสียงตรี)
Rising	sǐang jàt-dtà-waa	(เสียงจัตวา)

'sǐang' (เสียง) refers to the actual tone sound, not to the tone marks or tone rules that may be used in the syllable.

While the tone names are similar to the tone mark names, they do not refer to the same thing. For example, the tone mark 'mái èek' (ไม้เอก) may generate the tone sound 'sǐang too' (เสียงโท) depending on the consanant class.

Thai Numbers

๐	ศูนย์	0
๑	หนึ่ง	1
๒	สอง	2
๓	สาม	3
๔	สี่	4
๕	ห้า	5
๖	หก	6
๗	เจ็ด	7
๘	แปด	8
๙	เก้า	9

Days of the Week

day	wan วัน
Sunday	wan-aa-tít วันอาทิตย์
Monday	wan-jan วันจันทร์
Tuesday	wan-angkaan วันอังคาร
Wednesday	wan-pút วันพุธ
Thursday	wan-pá-rú-hàt วันพฤหัส
Friday	wan-sùk วันศุกร์
Saturday	wan-sǎo วันเสาร์
holiday	wan-yùt วันหยุด
weekend	sǎo-aa-tít เสาร์อาทิตย์

Months

month	dɯan เดือน
January	má-gà-raa (kom) มกรา (คม)
February	gumpaa (pan) กุมภา (พันธ์)
March	mii-naa (kom) มีนา (คม)
April	mee-sǎa (yon) เมษา (ยน)
May	prútsà-paa (kom) พฤษภา (คม)
June	mí-tù-naa (yon) มิถุนา (ยน)
July	gà-rá-gà-daa (kom) กรกฎา (คม)
August	sǐnghǎa (kom) สิงหา (คม)
September	gan-yaa (yon) กันยา (ยน)
October	dtù-laa (kom) ตุลา (คม)
November	prútsà-jì-gaa (yon) พฤศจิกา (ยน)
December	tan-waa (kom) ธันวา (คม)

Time

What time is it?	wee-laa tâo-rài?
	เวลาเท่าไหร่?
	gìi moong (lέεo)?
	กี่โมง (แล้ว)?
	gìi tûm (lέεo)?
	(at night only)
	กี่ทุ่ม (แล้ว)?

a.m.	1:00	dtii nừng	ตีหนึ่ง
	2:00	dtii sɔ̌ɔng	ตีสอง
	3:00	dtii sǎam	ตีสาม
	4:00	dtii sìi	ตีสี่
	5:00	dtii hâa	ตีห้า

6:00   hòk moong (cháao)   หกโมง (เช้า)

7:00   jèt moong (cháao) / (nừng) moong (cháao)
เจ็ดโมง (เช้า)/ (หนึ่ง)โมงเช้า

8:00   bpὲεt moong (cháao) / sɔ̌ɔng moong (cháao)
แปดโมง (เช้า) /สองโมง (เช้า)

9:00   gâao moong (cháao) / sǎam moong (cháao)
เก้าโมง (เช้า) /สามโมง (เช้า)

10:00   sìp moong (cháao) / sìi moong (cháao)
สิบโมง (เช้า) /สี่โมง (เช้า)

11:00   sìp-èt moong (cháao) / hâa moong (cháao)
สิบเอ็ดโมง (เช้า) /ห้าโมง (เช้า)

p.m. 12:00 tîang/tîang-wan / dtɔɔn tîang
เที่ยง / เที่ยงวัน / ตอนเที่ยง

1:00 bàai nùng (moong)/ bàai moong
บ่ายหนึ่ง (โมง) / บ่ายโมง

2:00 (bàai) sɔ̌ɔng moong (บ่าย) สองโมง

3:00 (bàai) sǎam moong (บ่าย) สามโมง

4:00 (bàai) sìi moong / sìi moong yen
(บ่าย) สี่โมง/ สี่โมงเย็น

5:00 (bàai) hâa moong / hâa moong yen
(บ่าย) ห้าโมง/ ห้าโมงเย็น

6:00 hòk moong (yen) หกโมง (เย็น)

7:00 (nùng) tûm (หนึ่ง) ทุ่ม

8:00 sɔ̌ɔng tûm สองทุ่ม

9:00 sǎam tûm สามทุ่ม

10:00 sìi tûm สี่ทุ่ม

11:00 hâa tûm ห้าทุ่ม

a.m. 12:00 hòk tûm/tîang-kʉʉn หกทุ่ม/ เที่ยงคืน

11:00 sìp-èt naa-lí-gaa* สิบเอ็ดนาฬิกา

20:00 yîi-sìp naa-lí-gaa* ยี่สิบนาฬิกา

*official

Note: There are many ways to tell time in Thai. You may not want to use them all at first. However, you will still need to understand the various forms when you hear them.

Colloquial Thai divides the 24 hour clock into four 6 hour blocks. One o'clock and seven o'clock are both one o'clock in this system; two o'clock and 8 o'clock are both 2 o'clock, etc. (this holds true for both a.m. and p.m.). The 24 hour military time system is also used, especially for official announcements (e.g. radio, train stations, airports).

Colors

color	sǐi สี
black	sǐi dam สีดำ
brown	sǐi náam-dtaan สีน้ำตาล
dark blue	sǐi náam-ngən สีน้ำเงิน
green	sǐi kǐao สีเขียว
grey	sǐi tao สีเทา
light blue	sǐi fáa สีฟ้า
pink	sǐi chompuu สีชมพู
purple	sǐi mûang สีม่วง
orange	sǐi sôm สีส้ม
red	sǐi dɛɛng สีแดง
white	sǐi kǎao สีขาว
yellow	sǐi lǔang สีเหลือง

Family Terms

family	krɔ̂ɔpkrua ครอบครัว
man, male	pûu-chaai ผู้ชาย
woman, female	pûu-yǐng ผู้หญิง
adult	pûu-yài ผู้ใหญ่
child	dèk/lûuk เด็ก/ลูก
son	lûukchaai ลูกชาย
daughter	lûuksǎao ลูกสาว
husband	sǎa-mii สามี
wife	pan-rá-yaa ภรรยา
husband (colloquial)	pǔa ผัว
wife (colloquial)	mia เมีย

father	pɔ̂ɔ พ่อ
mother	mɛ̂ɛ แม่
older sibling	pîi พี่
younger sibling	nɔ́ɔng น้อง
older brother	pîi-chaai พี่ชาย
older sister	pîi-sǎao พี่สาว
younger brother	nɔ́ɔng-chaai น้องชาย
younger sister	nɔ́ɔng-sǎao น้องสาว
father's father	bpùu ปู่
father's mother	yâa ย่า
mother's father	dtaa ตา
mother's mother	yaai ยาย
father or mother's older brother	lung ลุง
father or mother's older sister	bpâa ป้า
mother's younger brother or sister	náa น้า
father's younger brother or sister	aa อา

Names

Most Thai people have nicknames in addition to their official names. The nicknames do not necessarily come from their official names. When you know them well, Thai people prefer to be called by their nicknames. If they are close enough to you or younger than you, they may call themselves by their nicknames instead of using other pronouns.

Some Thai nicknames have meanings, and some don't. Treat them as mere names—don't try to translate the names because some might be funny or not make any sense.

Some Common Thai Nicknames

เล็ก	lék	น้อย	nɔ́ɔi	หน่อย	nɔ̀i
ใหญ่	yài	แดง	dɛɛng	ดำ	dam
ตุ๊กตา	dtùk-dtaa	แหม่ม	mɛ̀m	หมู	mǔu
ไก่	gài	หนึ่ง	nɨ̀ng	เป็ด	bpèt
แมว	mɛɛo	เหมียว	mǐao	แก้ว	gɛ̂ɛo
กุ้ง	gûng	นก	nók	หนู	nǔu
มด	mót	กบ	gòp	เอ๋	ěe
อั้น	ǎn	โอ๋	ǒo	เปี๊ยก	bpíak
แจง	jɛɛng	เจี๊ยบ	jíap	นุช	nút
ติ๋ม	dtǐm	ต้อย	dtɔ̂i	นิด	nít
ใหม่	mài	จิ๋ม	jǐm	หนิง	nǐng
บุ๋ม	bǔm	ติ๊ก	dtík	จุ๋ม	jǔm
เปิ้ล	bpên	โต้ง	dtôong	ตุ้ย	dtúi
ตุ๋ย	dtǔi	ส้ม	sôm	โจ้	jôo
ฝน	fǒn	ฟ้า	fáa	อ้อ	ɔ̂ɔ
แอน	ɛɛn	เดือน	dtɨan	ต้น	dtón
ติ๋ง	dtǐng	อุ๋ย	ǔi	อู๊ด	úut

Some Common Thai First Names

Thai has many first names. Here are some common ones that you can practice reading.

กมล	gà-mon	กรรณิการ์	ganní-gaa
กาญจนา	gaanjà-naa	เกษม	gà-sĕem
เกรียงศักดิ์	griang-sàk	ขวัญชัย	kwǎn-chai
จรัญ	jà-ran	จารุวรรณ	jaa-rú-wan
จินตนา	jin-dtà-naa	ฉวีวรรณ	chà-wǐi-wan
ชัยชาญ	chai-chaan	ชำนาญ	chamnaan
ดวงใจ	duang-jai	ดารณี	daa-rá-nii
ดำรงค์	damrong	ถนอม	tà-nɔ̌ɔm
ถาวร	tǎa-wɔɔn	ทนงศักดิ์	tá-nong-sàk
ทัศนีย์	tátsà-nii	ธงชัย	tong-chai
ธวัช	tá-wát	ธานี	taa-nii
ธิดา	tí-daa	นคร	ná-kɔɔn
ณรงค์	ná-rong	นงลักษณ์	nong-lák
นพดล	nóppá-don	นฤมล	ná-rú-mon
นวลจันทร์	nuanjan	นิคม	ní-kom
นิตยา	nít-dtà-yaa	บัญชา	banchaa
บุญชู	bunchuu	เบญจวรรณ	benjà-wan
ประกิต	bprà-gìt	ประจักษ์	bprà-jàk
ประชา	bprà-chaa	ประทุม	bprà-tum
ประไพ	bprà-pai	ประภา	bprà-paa
บัญญา	bpan-yaa	ปราณี	bpraa-nii
ปรีชา	bprii-chaa	พงศักดิ์	pongsàk
พรชัย	pɔɔnchai	พรทิพย์	pɔɔntíp
พรรณี	pannii	พิชัย	pí-chai

เพ็ญศรี	pensǐi	ไพบูลย์	paiboon
ไพโรจน์	pai-rôot	มนตรี	mon-dtrii
มนัส	má-nát	มยุรี	má-yú-rii
มานี	maa-nii	มานะ	maa-ná
มานิตย์	maa-nít	มาลี	maa-lii
ยุพา	yú-paa	ยุพิน	yú-pin
รัชนี	rátchá-nii	รัตนา	rát-dtà-naa
ละมัย	lá-mai	ลัดดา	látdaa
วัฒนา	wáttá-naa	วรรณี	wannii
วราภรณ์	wá-raa-pɔɔn	วันเพ็ญ	wanpen
วาสนา	wâatsà-nǎa	วิเชียร	wí-chian
วิชัย	wí-chai	วิทยา	wít-tá-yaa
วินัย	wí-nai	วิโรจน์	wí-rôt
วิไล	wí-lai	วิสุทธิ์	wí-sùt
วีระชัย	wii-rá-chai	ศราวุธ	sà-raa-wút
ศศิธร	sà-sì-tɔɔn	ศิริชัย	sì-rì-chai
ศิริพร	sì-rì-pɔɔn	ศักดา	sàkdaa
สกล	sà-gon	สมใจ	sǒmjai
สมชาย	sǒmchaai	สมชัย	sǒmchai
สมทรง	sǒmsong	สมพร	sǒmpɔɔn
สมพงษ์	sǒmpong	สมหมาย	sǒmmǎai
สมศรี	sǒm-sǐi	สมศักดิ์	sǒmsàk
สวัสดิ์	sà-wàt	สำราญ	sǎmraan
สุกัญญา	sù-gan-yaa	สุชาดา	sù-chaa-daa
สุชาติ	sù-châat	สุดา	sù-daa
สุทัศน์	sù-tát	สุเทพ	sù-têep
สุธรรม	sù-tam	สุนันท์	sù-nan

สุนันทา	sù-nan-taa	สุนีย์	sù-nii
สุพจน์	sù-pót	สุภา	sù-paa
สุภาภรณ์	sù-paa-pɔɔn	สุรชัย	sù-rá-chai
สุวรรณ	sù-wan	สุวรรณา	sù-wannaa
สุวิทย์	sù-wít	โสภา	sŏo-paa
ไสว	sà-wǎi	อดิศักดิ์	à-dì-sàk
อดุลย์	à-dun	อนงค์	à-nong
อนันต์	à-nan		

Some English Names Transliterated Into Thai

Here is how some English names are written in Thai. With foreign names, tones are sometimes pronounced differently from the way they are written.

Alan	อลัน	Albert	อัลเบิร์ต
Alex	อเล็กซ์	Ann	แอน
Anna	แอนนา	Barbara	บาร์บาร่า
Barry	แบรี่	Becky	เบ็กกี้
Beth	เบธ	Betty	เบตตี้
Bill	บิล	Bob	บ๊อบ
Bobby	บ๊อบบี้	Brian	ไบรอัน
Bruce	บรูซ	Caren/Karen	แคเรน
Carol/Carrol	แครอล	Charlie	ชาลี
Cherry	เชอรี่	Chris	คริส
Christina	คริสตืน่า	Connie	คอนนี่
Craig	เคร้ก	Dan	แดน
Daniel	แดนเนียล	Dave	เดฟ
David	เดวิด	Debbie	เดบบี้
Denny	เดนนี	Dick	ดิ๊ก
Don	ดอน	Donna	ดอนน่า
Earl	เอิร์ล	Eric	เอริค
Eva	อีวา	Eve	อีฟ
Frank	แฟรงค์	Fred	เฟรด
Gary	แกรี่	George	จอร์จ
Hal	แฮล	Harry	แฮรี่
Helen	เฮเลน	Isaac	ไอแซค
Jack	แจ๊ค	James	เจมส์
Jane	เจน	Janet	เจเน็ต

Jeffrey	เจฟฟรี่	Jennifer	เจนนิเฟอร์
Jerry	เจอรี่	Jenny	เจนนี่
Jessy	เจสซี่	Jinny	จินนี่
Jim	จิม	Jimmy	จิมมี่
Joe	โจ	Joey	โจอี้
John	จอห์น	Johnny	จอห์นนี่
Jody	โจดี้	Judy	จูดี้
Julie	จูลี่	Kate	เคท
Kathy	แคตี้	Kelly	เคลลี่
Ken	เคน	Kevin	เควิน
Kim	คิม	Larry	แลรี่
Linda	ลินดา	Lindsay	ลินซี่
Lisa	ลิซ่า	Lora	ลอร่า
Lori	ลอรี่	Mark	มาร์ค
Mary	แมรี่	Michael	ไมเคิล
Michelle	มิเชล	Nancy	แนนซี่
Pam	แพม	Pat	แพท
Paul	พอล, ปอล	Paula	พอลล่า
Peter	ปีเตอร์	Philip	ฟีลิป
Randy	แรนดี้	Richard	ริชาร์ด
Rick	ริค	Robert	โรเบิร์ต
Ron	รอน	Ruth	รูธ, รูท
Sam	แซม	Sandra	แซนดร้า
Sandy	แซนดี้	Scott	สกอต
Steve	สตีฟ	Stephanie	สเตฟานี
Sue	ซู	Susan/Suzanne	ซูซาน
Tim	ทิม	Tom	ทอม
Tony	โทนี่	Tricia	ทริเชีย
William	วิลเลียม	Wymond	วายมอนด์

Some Common Thai Dishes

ต้มยำกุ้ง	dtôm-yamgûng	lemon grass shrimp soup
ต้มข่าไก่	dtômkàa-gài	galanga chicken soup
แกงจืด	gɛɛng-jʉ̀ʉt	mild soup with vegetables & pork
ยำเนื้อ	yamnʉ́a	spicy beef salad
ยำวุ้นเส้น	yamwúnsên	bean thread salad
ยำมะเขือ	yammá-kʉ̌a	spicy eggplant salad
ลาบเนื้อ	lâapnʉ́a	spicy beef salad
ส้มตำ	sôm-dtam	spicy green papaya salad
ปอเปี๊ยะ	bpɔɔ-bpía	spring rolls
สะเต๊ะ	sà-dté	satay
แกงเผ็ด	gɛɛng-pèt	curry, red curry
แกงเขียวหวาน	gɛɛng-kǐao-wǎan	green curry
แกงป่า	gɛɛng-bpàa	country style curry
แกงส้ม	gɛɛng-sôm	sour fish curry
ไก่ย่าง	gài-yâang	chicken barbecue
ไก่ผัดขิง	gài-pàtkǐng	fried chicken with ginger
กุ้งผัดพริกเผา	gûng-pàtpríkpǎo	fried prawn with chillies
ปลาหมึกผัดเผ็ด	bplaa-mùk pàt-pèt	spicy fried squid
ขนมจีน	kà-nǒmjiin	Thai vermicilli
ผัดเปรี้ยวหวาน	pàt-bprîao-waan	fried sweet and sour
ผัดไทย	pàt-tai	Thai fried noodles
ข้าวผัด	kâao-pàt	fried rice
ข้าวผัดกุ้ง	kâao-pàtgûng	fried rice with shrimp

ข้าวสวย kâao-sŭai   steamed rice

ข้าวเหนียว kâao-nĭao   sticky rice

ข้าวต้ม kâao-dtôm   rice porridge

ข้าวต้มหมู kâao-dtômmŭu   rice porridge with pork

ไข่เจียว kài-jiao   omelette

ไข่ดาว kài-daao   sunny side-up

ไข่ต้ม kài-dtôm   boiled egg

Desserts ของหวาน kŏɔng-wăan

ข้าวเหนียวมะม่วง   sticky rice with mango
  kâao-nĭao-má-mûang

สะหริ่ม sà-rìm   jelly pea flour with coconut
                                       milk

ตะโก้ dtà-gôo   Thai jelly with coconut
                                       cream

ข้าวหลาม kâao-lăam   sticky rice and coconut in
                                       bamboo

ข้าวเหนียวดำ kâao-nĭao-dam   black rice pudding

กล้วยบวชชี glûai-bùatchii   banana in coconut milk

กล้วยเชื่อม glûai-chûam   banana stewed in syrup

สังขยา săng-kà-yăa   coconut custard

หม้อแกง mɔ̂ɔ-gɛɛng   egg custard

ฝอยทอง fɔ̆ɔi-tɔɔng   sweet shredded egg yolk

ไอติม/ไอสครีม ai-dtim/ai-sà-kriim   ice cream

Thai Language Books by Paiboon Publishing

Title: **Thai for Beginners**
Author: Benjawan Poomsan Becker ©1995
Description: Designed for either self-study or classroom use. Teaches all four language skills— speaking, listening (when used in conjunction with the cassette tapes), reading and writing . Offers clear, easy, step-by-step instruction building on what has been previously learned. Used by many Thai temples and insitutes in America. Cassette tapes available. Paperback. 262 pages. 6" x 8.5"

Book US$12.95 Stock # 1001
Three Tape Set US$20.00 Stock # 1001T

****

Title: **Thai for Intermediate Learners**
Author: Benjawan Poomsan Becker ©1998
Description: The continuation of *Thai for Beginners* . Users are expected to be able to read basic Thai language. There is transliteration when new words are introduced. Teaches reading, writing and speaking at a higher level. Keeps students interested with cultural facts about Thailand. Helps expand your Thai vocabulary in a systematic way. Two casettes available. Paperback. 220 pages. 6" x 8.5"

Book US$12.95 Stock # 1002
Two Tape Set US$15.00 Stock # 1002T

****

Title: **Thai for Advanced Readers**
Author: Benjawan Poomsan Becker ©2000
Description: A book that helps students practice reading Thai at an advanced level. It contains reading exercises, short essays, newspaper articles, cutural and historical facts about Thailand and miscellaneous information about the Thai language. Students need to be able to read basic Thai. Two casette tapes available. Paperback. 210 pages. 6" x 8.5"

Book US$12.95 Stock # 1003
Two Tape Set US$15.00 Stock # 1003T

****

Title: **Thai for Lovers**
Author: Nit & Jack Ajee ©1999
Description: An ideal book for lovers. A short cut to romantic communication in Thailand. There are useful sentences with their Thai translations throughout the book. You won't find any Thai language book more fun and user-friendly. **Rated R!** Two casettes available. Paperback. 190 pages. 6" x 8.5"

Book US$13.95 Stock #: 1004
Two Tape Set US$17.00 Stock #: 1004T

Title:	**Thai for Gay Tourists**
Author:	Saksit Pakdeesiam ©2001
Description:	The ultimate language guide for gay and bisexual men visiting Thailand. Lots of gay oriented language, culture, commentaries and other information. Instant sentences for convenient use by gay visitors. Fun and sexy. The best way to communicate with your Thai gay friends and partners! **Rated R!**

Cassette tapes available. Paperback. 220 pages. 6" x 8.5"

| Book | US$13.95 | Stock # 1007 |
| Two Tape Set | US$17.00 | Stock # 1007T |

****

Deutschsprachiges Lehrbuch über die Thai-Sprache von Paiboon Publishing

Titel:	**Thai für Anfänger**
Autor:	Benjawan Poomsan Becker ©2000
Beschreibung:	Für das selbständige Lernen zu Hause oder für den Gebrauch im Klassenzimmer. Vermittelt Grundkenntnisse der Thai-Sprache. Das Buch kann mit den entsprechenden Tonbandkassetten kombiniert werden. Bietet klare und einfache Instruktionen, die Schritt für Schritt auf bereits Erlerntem aufbauen. Wird von zahlreichen Thai-Tempeln und Sprachinstituten in Amerika benutzt.

Tonbandkassetten erhältlich. Taschenbuch. 245 Seiten. 15 cm x 22 cm

| Buch | US$13.95 | Lagernummer | 1005 |
| Kassetten (3er Set) | US$20.00 | Lagernummer | 1005T |

****

All books are fun and easy to use.
Mit unseren Büchern macht das Lernen Spass.

PAIBOON PUBLISHING
ORDER FORM

QTY.	ITEM NO.	NAME OF ITEM	ITEM PRICE	TOTAL

| | | Merchandise Total | |
| Merchandise Total | | | |

Delivery Charges for First Class and Airmail

	USA and Canada	Other Countries
Up to $25.00	US$3.95	US$8.95
$25.01-$50.00	US$4.95	US$11.95
$50.01-$75.00	US$6.25	US$15.25
$75.01-$100.00	US$7.75	US$18.75
Over $100.00	FREE	US$18.75

Merchandise Total

CA residents add 8.25% sales tax

Delivery Charge (See Chart at Left)

Total

Method of Payment ❒ Check ❒ Money Order Make payable to Paiboon Publishing

Charge to: ❒ Visa ❒ Master Card ❒ Amex

Card # _____ Exp. Date ____ / ____

Signature_____ Tel _____

Name _____ Date _____

Address _____

_____

_____

Email Address _____

Mail order is for orders outside of Thailand only.
Send your order and payment to: Paiboon Publishing
PMB 192, 1442A Walnut Street, Berkeley, CA 94709 USA
Tel: 1-510-848-7086 Fax: 1-510-848-4521
Email: paiboon@thailao.com Website: www.thailao.com
Allow 2-3 weeks for delivery.

PAIBOON
PP
PUBLISHING

Please send us your comments.

We hope you have enjoyed using this book. We want to make it even better for you. If you would like to offer some advice or updated information, please send your comments to Paiboon Publishing with your contact information. If your comments are selected for inclusion in our next edition, we will send you a free copy of the next edition of *Thai for Lovers*. Please use extra paper if needed. Comments can be sent by mail, email and fax. Thank you.

_____

_____

_____

_____

_____

_____

_____

_____

_____

Name _____

Address _____

_____

_____

Email Address _____

Phone Number _____

November 2004 [4802-034/2,000(2)]